PANDORA'S

BALL

By

EDWARD S. BICKER

Dedication

I wish to dedicate this book to my mother, my family, my friends, and many teachers who always told me I can. I also want to dedicate this, and all my work, to the bullies in my life who told me I can't.

Acknowledgment

So many people inspired me to acknowledge each of them individually, and I'd hate to leave anybody out. Instead, I will thank the indomitable spirit of the truth movement. This spirit has thankfully infected me.

Table of Contents

Preface

I am inspired to help undo problems caused by mass deception. Hopefully, this book will serve as a contribution. As I navigated my way through young adulthood, I was introduced to the world of *questioning authority*. A friend introduced me to the idea that the government was in lockstep with the media. Both serve as authorities. Subsequently, I came to understand there is a metaphorical rabbit hole of corruption, which can only exist in the absence of truth. In this book, I will introduce a truth that will obliterate this world of corruption.

This book shares much of the knowledge I gained from more than three decades of researching society's political fringe. I do not claim to be among those who discovered eye-opening conspiracies, but rather a conduit exercising his duty-based ethics. The information in this book will acquaint the reader with the mechanisms and power of controlled information.

This work is not about assigning personal blame for society's problems. Instead, it's meant to help readers recognize and step beyond the powerful influence of media and other controlling forces. Structured as a journey down a figurative rabbit hole, it invites you to explore deeper truths and question the narratives that guide the direction of our lives.

It's worth noting that the depths reached in this book are the depths reached by the author so far. I have sourced appropriately, but I strongly recommend that the reader conduct further research on everything discussed in this book. Information is more available today than at any other time in history.

Introduction

"It's easier to fool somebody than it is to convince them they were fooled," *Mark Twain*.

We'll start with acknowledging that this quote may apply to: Media, formal education, government, medicine, religion, and cosmology.

Time, energy, and emotional commitments invested in beliefs often cause people to cling to them, even in the face of strong contrary evidence. Beyond the sting of being wrong, many people seek approval, but overreliance on external validation leaves them vulnerable to exploitation.

Popularity is a signal that a given behavior is the best choice. There is a <u>heuristic</u> most of us use to determine what to do, think, say, and buy: the principle of social proof. To learn what is correct, we look at what other people are doing. In his bestselling book *Influence: The Psychology of Persuasion*, psychologist Robert Cialdini writes:

> *"Whether the question is what to do with an empty popcorn box in a movie theater, how fast to drive on a certain stretch of highway, or how to eat the chicken at a dinner party, the actions of those around us will be important in defining the answer."*

Social proof is a shortcut to deciding how to act.[1]

The terms **"red pill"** and **"blue pill"** refer to a choice between the willingness to learn a potentially unsettling or

---

[1] The Science Behind Why People Follow the Crowd | Psychology Today

life-changing truth by taking the red pill or remaining in contented ignorance with the blue pill.

In *The Matrix*, the main character , Neo, is offered the choice between a red pill and a blue pill by rebel leader Morpheus. Morpheus says, "You take the blue pill... the story ends, you wake up in your bed and believe whatever you want to believe. You take the red pill... you stay in Wonderland, and I show you how deep the rabbit hole goes."

The red pill represents an uncertain future, unknown to Neo at the time. If he takes the red pill, it would free him from the enslaving control of the machine-generated dream world and allow him to escape into the real world. However, living the "truth of reality" is harsher and more difficult. On the other hand, the blue pill represents a beautiful prison—it would lead him back to ignorance, living in confined comfort without want or fear within the simulated reality of the Matrix. Neo chooses the red pill and joins the rebellion.[2]

Taking the blue pill seems more appealing to those contented with their status and material luxuries. The red pill offers nothing additional in a non-spiritual sense. However, as worldwide volatility becomes more inescapable due to the prevalence of massive lies, the blue pill's effectiveness wears off. At some point, we must all consider the red pill. The red pill is as addictive as the truth.

Oftentimes, the red pill need not be taken by choice. Great boxer Mike Tyson once said, "Everyone has a plan

---

[2] Red pill and blue pill - Wikipedia

until they get punched in the mouth."[3] In boxing, they say it's the punch you don't see coming that knocks you out. In the wider world, the reality we ignore or deny is the one that weakens our most impassioned efforts toward improvement. – Katherine Dunn .[4]

The red pill may come to us due to a life-altering experience or out of innate curiosity. Such is the idiom reality-check. Each person gets these from time to time, but when you overinvest in a false perception, your crash is more severe. It is reality, not gravity, that brings us back down to Earth.

Hundreds of words and phrases are categorized as "good" or "bad" by consistently adding a narrative to the word. The underlying narrative tells the reader or viewer that they must dismiss being objective wherever these words appear. The latter is regardless of the word's definition. I've noticed a plethora of "conspiracy theorist" attachments to the use of red pill analogies.

In an online article called *The Matrix: how conspiracy theorists hijacked the 'red pill' philosophy*, the author claims that "One of The Matrix's most enduring cultural contributions has been to conspiracy theories,"[5]

---

[3] "Everybody has a plan until they get punched in the mouth." - How did the famous Mike Tyson quote originate? (sportskeeda.com)

[4] In boxing, they say it's the punch you don't see coming that knocks you out. In the wider world, the reality we ignore or deny is the one that weakens our (allgreatquotes.com)

[5] The Matrix: how conspiracy theorists hijacked the 'red pill' philosophy (theconversation.com)

But a conspiracy theorist cannot hijack the red pill philosophy. The red pill would eliminate conspiracy theories unless they were true and not based on prejudices.

The term [conspiracy theory] has a negative connotation, implying that the appeal to a conspiracy is based on prejudice or insufficient evidence [confirmation bias]. Conspiracy theories resist falsification and are reinforced by circular reasoning: both evidence against the conspiracy and an absence of evidence for it are re-interpreted as evidence of its truth, whereby the conspiracy becomes a matter of faith rather than something that can be proven or disproven.[6] Often, the "evidence" against the conspiracy is the rampant money spent to suppress it. Media parrots, paid scientists, politicians, and "eye witnesses" are consistently used to verify political narratives every day.

So, if there is a Matrix, who designed it? Is it a person atop an organized hierarchy, an alien being, or is the designer not even tangible? Evil is a negative force that can be unfollowed. My nugget from the classic movie *The Wizard of Oz,* as the Good Witch explained to Dorothy at the end, was that the solution to our problems is inside us. What is outside of us is an illusion. Many of us spend too much of our lives outwardly focused.

The illusion of an honest and unbiased news **media** is gradually wearing off. However, television remains the number one hobby for the vast majority of people. Though the **government** is not an illusion per se, when the government outgrows its value, there is delusional

---

[6] Conspiracy theory - Wikipedia

authoritarianism. **Medicine** is emphasized in an unhealthy society. **Religion** is as good as the spirituality within the congregation. This book will navigate through these segments of society's troubling rabbit hole. If the reader is intrigued to venture even deeper, he will discover an Earth-shattering predicament.

I

The Means of Mass Communication

A friend once told me, "Ed, it's *Tinseltown*." Unbeknownst to me at the time, that was so spot on.

Most people flock to their televisions, cell phones, radios, and computers to get their daily dose of local, national, and world current events without realizing that their attention is being redirected by design. The news. Thousands of stories qualify as newsworthy, but those who own the media choose which ones the audience will see and hear. The owners also hire and fire in accordance with who is best able to present a narrative. The news and entertainment industry is carefully managed. Many people consider large portions of it morally unacceptable, but most of these viewers have not connected the dots. The lyrics in the middle of the Bee Gees' 1977 hit song *Stayin' Alive*, "But we can try to understand the New York Times' effect on man"[7] are spoken so fast that most people do not comprehend the words. Most people also do not understand the effect the *New York Times* has on men.

No influence is greater than that of those who control information. Information causes behavior. A picture is worth a thousand words, and an accompanying news headline can exponentialize the impact: defamation or adulation. The media is an encoded message, and the decoding is up to the viewer. While it's true that all media is biased in accordance

---

[7] Bee Gees – Stayin' Alive Lyrics | Genius Lyrics

with the author and editor, the media that reaches the greatest audience has the greatest effectiveness. The owners of television networks, newspapers, radio stations, and Internet companies are the policymakers of mass communication information. Part of the ownership policy is to hide this simple fact to preserve their influence. The marketed appearance of open-mindedness is a feature of all media.

Television sits atop the mass-conditioning chain, with almost all Western households turning it on every day. Aside from the few who completely understand that television is a source of unhealthy information, the audience allows their reality to be manipulated. Emotions spill over when we see graphic details of an apparent unjust event that our firsthand senses have never experienced.

Imagine owning a fine restaurant with a growing customer base. Now imagine the restaurant down the street struggling to break even. Your opposition, however, has close connections to the media. A phone call is made, and your restaurant gets a visit from a food safety agency, and the visit makes the local news. The next morning's newspaper headline reads, "Food Safety Inspectors Find a Possible Food Safety Violation at *Your Restaurant*." One headline, a hundred fewer customers. Note that the headline does not even mean the restaurant is unsafe to eat at. Now, suppose a candidate for office is polling a few points behind his opponent, and the network owners favor his candidacy. The network broadcasts an undesirable story about the leading candidate, and opinion is swayed. That's the power of the media.

Where a headline shows an aggressor, the publication is asking for support to oppose. An indictment. If they can secure the indictment, subsequent action instructions will follow. Problem→reaction→solution. This tactic has been used by war hawks for centuries, and is not slowing down now. What seems to be slowing down is the readiness to accept the information provided. Erosion of trust is what happens to habitual liars.

Much of the media is true on its face. From a cynical standpoint, it has to be. The weather, sports scores, starting times for various events, and many stories around town are shared facts. The media is also segmented to encourage broad audience participation, which is why there are different networks supporting different perspectives. However, there are shared parameters even when it comes to opinions on different networks. The latter is particularly true of the legacy media. Television creates the fringe.

Freedom of speech and freedom of the press are important. So, even when there is bias, civil rights are to be protected. Viewers need to understand the difference between an opinion and a fact. Moreover, even when there are facts presented in the media, the story is still quite often incomplete.

The print media, particularly chain newspapers, once rivaled television in their ability to persuade. The same principles were applied throughout their successful reign. However, newspapers are in their declining stage of the life cycle. The Internet is far more convenient than dragging a bulky newspaper around, and news stories can be archived online instantly. Nonetheless, it is important to note that while newspapers were in their growth and maturity phases, they corroborated the vast majority of what is seen on television and Internet conglomerates today. Newspapers played a significant role in shaping the minds of the masses who were born in the middle of the last century. The transition to television at a subconscious level was pretty easy. Television piggybacked off the information already installed in the minds of the masses.

The wild card in the media manipulation game is the Internet. Individual opinions are voiced and easily archivable on virtually countless platforms. The playing field is still not level, but many people are turning to alternate sources of information because the parameters of acceptability are widened to allow dissident political perspectives, which is also a basic right of freedom. Much of the legacy media censors free speech away, either subtly or with indignation. There has been a long-standing undercurrent of resentment toward the media for decades. Television propaganda may have reached its zenith. If so, its death phase will be welcomed by many who feel misrepresented.

A relatively new slogan has entered the consciousness of many people who once blindly believed in television and big tech companies. "Fake news" was used as a phrase by Donald Trump throughout his 2016 Presidential campaign, and multiple times daily ever since. If President Trump wasn't deliberately awakening the masses to biased news reporting, his incidental rants served just as well.

As people become increasingly disappointed with the television network's biases and choose to get their information online, television "programming" becomes less effective. Big Tech companies have countered by taking over much of the information online as well, and now use techno-savviness to utilize algorithms for censorship. People are catching on to that maneuver now as well. So, the question is what is being censored and why?

Obviously, certain perspectives should be censored if they contain illegal or violent activity. But what about information that doesn't, but may seem far-fetched? Notice how big tech companies now have certain "community standards," a vague description of what is acceptable viewership. In other words, there is a rather significant effort to erase non-conformity from the tech world.

Digressing back to television, the whole concept of modern media caring about what impressionable young viewers watch holds nearly zero merit. Whilst aggressively censoring political dissidence, the media pours out countless scenes of deadly violence, infidelity, and an array of unhealthy activities every hour of every day. The average child sees thousands of violent acts on television annually. Relationships where sex is assumed between unmarried partners are shown 24 times more often than sex between spouses.[8]

At the end of the day, we never had to watch television. In fact, even if television had little or no violence or promiscuity, too much viewing would still be an unhealthy habit. Physical and spiritual laziness are both deadly sins.

---

[8] Children and the media - PMC (nih.gov)

II

Government ≠ Freedom

In 2001, I decided to run for a seat on the city council in my small community – rather insignificant in the whole scope of American politics. Walking from door to door, I was hoping to persuade any registered voter who answered to consider my candidacy. Listening more than talking was one of the instructions I received from my experienced friend. I added sincere eye contact to my act. I routed the last day of my door-to-door campaigning so I would wind up at my opponent's house, but I balked. I still remember the two-mile walk home when I heard little kids playing in their yard, "Olly, olly oxen free." The innocence contrasted with the nature of politics. My opponent had money, experience, and backing from the mayor. I did not get elected, but did I lose or win?

Privacy is the right to control personal information and maintain boundaries. This allows individuals to choose what to share and with whom.

Secrecy is intentionally withholding specific information for fear of scrutiny.

The claim is that governments have saved people from their propensity for self-destruction. There is no land anywhere without a government; hence, no significant sample-size data is available for a government versus anarchy hypothesis test. The only agreement is that if the test ever does become available, it would reject the null hypothesis. At its best, governments protect the citizens and allow those with bad luck to maintain an adequate lifestyle. Government at its worst morphs into an organized crime network.

The U.S. government is a privately funded political system. There is a direct correlation between campaign money spent and election success. Extensive campaign ads and the ability to defame are created with money. The larger and more important the office, the more money is needed. Funding candidates is a business investment. If a powerful industry funds a candidate who is relying on that funding, he or she will become a de facto employee. Once in office, the government official will almost always vote and enact legislation in accordance with their funding. Corporations buy legislation.

Governments organize a plethora of safety, conveniences, and educational services. Schools, courts, police, fire, emergency rescue teams, and military branches are all functions of modern governments. Services create and maintain adequate infrastructure. The educational system ensures that everyone attains the knowledge needed to thrive both individually and collectively. Considering the positives, can governments outgrow their usefulness?

Many books are filled with stories of tyrannical governments enslaving their populations and imprisoning or killing their dissidents. Governments in freer societies tend to allow for dissent. A good example of government growth parasitically is the United States. The U.S. Constitution was not constructed for the purpose of developing a sizeable government; *the Constitution was written so the people could control the government.* America's founders sought a system of autonomy free of micromanagement. Fast forward a couple of centuries, and the effects of bureaucratic infiltration are an American epidemic. Moreover, many of these bureaucracies harass small non-government businesses. Intimidating or beating up somebody weaker shows the character of the bully. Accepting authority out of fear makes the authority null and void.

For a government to operate, there must be initial consent. Once the consent is given, the power shifts from the people to the governors. This seems to be an endless historical cycle. The government starts out as a mechanism to ensure freedom, and then enthusiastically grows to contain it. The growth occurs because the government has been granted the ability to take the place of individual autonomy.

Governments always grow under the auspicious need of a greater good. Of course, the need angle is a public relations move to prevent or modify dissent. The larger the government grows, the less the concern about dissidence. The latter concept is exponentially more profound if the government can disarm the citizens. Whoever stated that the government grows like weeds is spot on. Weeds need to be trimmed periodically, or they will get out of control.

Even the staunchest libertarians agree that governments are necessary. Thomas Paine described government as a "necessary evil." Here, he describes government as "an institution whose primary role is to restrain people from indulging their evil natures."[9]

So, is government a necessity or an obstacle?

In many ways, governments are a business. They take in revenue and provide a service. The business life cycle is generally as follows: Launch, growth, maturity, decline, death. This seems to fit in perfectly with all past and present governments.

Launch: The government begins with an attractive organizational campaign to represent the interests of the people. People agree with dutifully building a defense to ensure their society remains free from outside exploitation. Law enforcement begins with a simple understanding of don't harm, cheat, or steal from your neighbor. A low-cost introductory tax base is developed.

Growth: Growth happens as goodwill spreads and the productive class is rewarded economically and spiritually. As the economic base grows, so does the need to protect it from outsiders. Add here and there to ensure the prosperity continues. As the growth continues, nepotism rears its head. The list of alphabet bureaucracies is supersized. The larger the government grows, the less the transparency. There is a federal government, state governments, county governments, and local governments. Along with these governments, there are millions of laws. The lawmakers are paid via taxation.

---

[9] Thomas Paine's "Government is A Necessary Evil" | Free Essay Example (studycorgi.com)

Maturity: Governments mature when there is a maximized tax base while maintaining legitimate amenities from the taxpayers. The government equilibrates taxing with social programs, foreign policy, and personal encroachment. These are all in tow with an affordable budget and acceptable personal infringements.

Decline: Once the first penny of deficit spending occurs, the decline has begun. A deficit is an unseen tax. The government overspends, and the time value of money dictates that interest will be added to the deficit. Denial from the government's spokespeople follows. Incumbent politicians cite a rising average income, but it's almost always due to the wealthiest getting wealthier. However, when the median income is adjusted for inflation, a factor that rarely receives airtime or political campaign attention, the up or down numbers demonstrate true economic health. Problem identifying and party bickering diverts attention away from the best solution. Government reduction never happens until it has to happen.

Death: The death of a nation usually happens when the working/producing population (the host) can no longer sustain the parasitic spenders in charge of the system. Governments also see a gradual moral decline from their modest roots. So far, all governments have reemerged in some form. However, many people see a paradigm shift coming at some point. Could the government, as a controlling body, see an apocalypse?

In order to maintain an expansive state, the government relies on trickery, which is undoubtedly why empires do not fall much sooner than they do. Their biggest trick is the illusion that they are the ones in power. In reality, it is the producers who are host to the parasites. Producers can live without the parasites, but parasites cannot live without a host. So, how does the government convince the population that it is needed and powerful?

When the government colludes with the means of mass communication, the currency institutions, and the educational system, its control is augmented. Organized religions are not free of government control. The banking industry works with the government to lend money at a population-group cost. The educational system writes and edits history.

Once the government locks in these powers, they flex their muscles. The impressive physique, built with PEDs, creates an atmosphere of fear. Even the politicians themselves lose the authority to lessen government control because they are replaceable. If they refuse to be metaphorically neutered, they will be attacked by their colleagues, the media, their financiers, and, ultimately, the very citizens they claim to represent.

Regardless of how much power governments accrue, true history has demonstrated they are all beholden to a finite timeline. Somewhere in the maturity phase of the life cycle, the government will laterally finger-point to give the illusion that citizen representation is being addressed. This way, the government can prolong its control. During the declining phase, the party not in control will blame the ones who are, and the media will enthusiastically join in on this promotion angle. It's always the "parties involved" rather than the system as a whole.

III

War: Lateral Violence Rather Than Subduing The Instigator

Can history books truly be filled with wars that were justified? Remember, only governments can start wars. Wars should never happen. Correct me if I'm wrong, but why send our youth out to kill and be killed until one too many on one side surrenders? In my lifetime, I have seen zero good come from all the murders and destruction that come from war. Did the Vietnam War make America or Vietnam better? Did the hundreds of thousands of non-combatant deaths and trillions just spent in Afghanistan and Iraq help the world? Governments create suffering in so many ways.

The so-called *defense* budget for 2023 was $816.7 billion.[10] Aircraft carriers, fighter jets, bombers, submarines, missiles, tanks, machine guns, bullets, lasers, etc., are used to kill people all over the world every day, sometimes by the U.S. and sometimes by its friends. There are hundreds of thousands of deaths every year from armed conflicts involving militaries.[11] Ponder that thought for a moment.

When there is a "mass" shooting in the U.S., it is headline news for weeks. The vast majority, if not all, of the shooters are not representative of the common American who values the Second Amendment. Although these shootings are tragic, the mass shootings usually involve

---

[10] Most expensive US military weapons and programs - What's Up Newp
[11] Deaths in armed conflicts, World

single-digit death counts, and the legislators are pressured into coming up with a way to disarm the citizens. These same legislators almost unanimously pass military budgets that create the most deadly and advanced weapons in the world, and then use them daily to kill innocent people.

Governments are supposed to be a reflection of the populations they represent, operating within established borders. Some governments buddy up with others who have similar doctrines. This was especially true throughout the twentieth century. There were two world wars when nations took sides to defeat commonly perceived enemies. Following the Second World War, there was a non-lethal battle. This was called the Cold War, where one side was led by the United States and the other side by the Soviet Union. The Western nations considered themselves governmentally superior to the communist bloc nations. Each side felt the need to show superiority. Military parades, Olympic events, and general propaganda always made headlines. Tensions continued, suggesting future violence was possibly unavoidable. Communism was eventually overthrown on its own merit, however.

Under the guise of morality, non-defensive wars are acts of violent aggression. The larger offending government ends up killing citizens in the "not-a-democracy" country at a more efficient rate than its dictator ever could. The latter results in countrywide suffering and instability. This is all accomplished with the inelastic military budget created out of recurrent fear.

There has never been a war that didn't have a better peaceful alternative. Mandatory compliance orders are given by cowards. Indeed, wars are launched in luxurious boardrooms and conference rooms by so-called "leaders," not by the teenagers who fight, bleed, and die on the front lines. Not to mention non-combatant deaths from vicious bombings. Somebody who wants to believe he is in charge of the lives and well-being of people he doesn't even know gives a war order, which is usually preceded by a marketing campaign. The order is then promoted and made official by the non-official mainstream media. For a war to reach the point of acceptability, there must be a real or perceived aggression, as well as a nation to assign the blame to. Wars then morph into an attempt to passionately disseminate the true aggressor's sociological system. Empire-building in foreign lands.

Absent from proper news coverage are the politicians who truly tout peace. Many people cite the Jimmy Carter legacy as a failed administration. "I was lucky enough when I was president to keep our country at peace and provide peace for others. I was lucky enough to go through my four years; we never dropped a bomb, we never fired a missile, we never shot a bullet."[12] Absent from history classes in America is the proposal for a U.S. Department of Peace from one of this nation's founders, Benjamin Rush.[13]

No peace without a democracy? This automatically assumes there is a higher moral law that is only found in democratic societies. Therefore, the goal must be to achieve a democracy, even if it means mass killing? How many

---

[12] (2) Jimmy Carter Never Dropped a Bomb Response to John McCain's Insult - YouTube
[13] ESSAY: "A Plan of a Peace-Office for the United States" by Benjamin Rush – Art & Theology

democracies in the world actually reflect the wishes of the majority? In reality, democracies are more or less tyrannies, bullying a significant portion of civilians to accept a law or forced tax they find wrong or burdensome. Anytime other people forbid you the discretion of your earnings, you are in bondage because the product of your labor belongs to your oppressors.

Democracies make policy based on a voting system with more than half of the votes, regardless of how that majority came to their conclusion. The authorities in democratic systems decide the parameters of a given issue. For example, should you be taxed 20% or 40%? Is that really fair to the minority? Are the majority of voters truly educated and experienced enough to cast a vote of equal value? What if they are not? What if the majority vote to have the minority perform around-the-clock slave labor? Now, consider it is minorities who overwhelmingly crave democracies. Clearly, many nations rightly do not like or agree with the tenets of democracies.

Not many historical events happen that are truly sadder than war. However, classrooms around the world are filled with depictions of national pride due to the conquering of an enemy via mass killing. A question that seems never to be widely asked is how many residents actually ever supported two nations sending their youths to butcher each other. Someone with too much control is telling the rest that there is a necessity for lifelong wars; otherwise, they just wouldn't happen. War is perpetrated by those who have no physical stake in the outcome.

Obviously, in order to create a mass conflict, there must be mass consent at a high spiritual level. Wars are always started with information. Starting back a century or so, newspapers, then radios, then televisions, then online information molded public perception into a state of fear, anger, and national pride. A similar kind of psychological manipulation is found in the acronym FOG (fear, obligation, guilt), coined by Susan Forward and Donna Frazier in *Emotional Blackmail*.[14] The controller in the relationship uses fog as a means to distort the victim's vision.

Major events around America often begin with the national anthem, *Star Spangled Banner*. The song subconsciously gives goosebumps to millions. The irony is that the lead-ins of war in the anthem are synonymous with violence. Mass violence shouldn't happen, yet it is glamorized. Though there's nothing wrong with self-defense, people dying violently is tragic.

Problem, reaction, solution. An action by an aggressor causes a problem leading to a chain reaction, and then a solution. The solution is to create a satellite government/puppet regime in the conquered land.

There will always be great admiration for the many people who dedicate their lives to ensuring others are safe. Past and present war veterans deserve gratitude for their bravery. The armchair antagonist veterans do not.

Most people honor and sympathize with lost veterans. However, an element of confusion surrounds the armed service members who dissent from active war duty. Popular

---

[14] FOG - Fear, Obligation & Guilt — Out of the FOG

opinion has it that if somebody volunteers for the military, he or she has a duty to follow orders from a superior. Though it is true that when an armed service person signs up for the military, it is also assumed that he or she may one day find the front lines of a conflict, the entire process implies that the conflict is legally justified. An anti-Constitutional war, one where there is no formal congressional approval, is not binding. Therefore, there is no justifiable recourse against conscientious objectors. The premise of a national defense is *to defend.*

The costs of war are high in terms of money and mortality, even for the "winners" of the war. How can a family that just lost their masculine leader for a cause that could have been settled in a benign manner believe they made a gain for it, even if they were financially compensated? There is often very negligible monetary compensation for veterans. The costs of the losing side are more dead and wounded, sunk financial costs, and a surrender to conditions from the opposing side. Besides the financial and mortality costs, the desensitizing of violent behavior that is created during wartime prepares the spirit for another and another. How many Hollywood shows feature heroes who reach their finest hour by killing fellow human beings?

Compared to the general population, those who engage in fierce war have several times more incidents of suicide and post-traumatic stress disorder (PTSD). Many war veterans have lifelong physical illnesses as well. The rippling financial effects of war include fewer resources elsewhere as well as the devaluation of currency. Funds used for wars are, in reality, clandestine taxes.

Enter the banking industry, the beneficiary of perennial war. International banks create money out of thin air, then loan it to both sides of the conflict. Both sides are subsequently indebted. The interest on those loans can become so high that entire nations remain in bondage for decades. The irony is that banks lent what they never actually possessed: fiat currency.

Obviously, if a country is attempting to free itself from tyranny and the only option is a standoff in the face of an oppressive army, then a strong case could be made to justify that action. Fighting for freedom is somewhere inside all of us. Moreover, the burden of guilt would be on the offending nation. In such cases, reparations on the part of those found guilty of the oppression could be considered fair and ideal.

The media bombards the public with good words and bad words, a tactic that has helped keep the "democracy" and "terrorist" paradigms afloat for decades. The establishment of democracy is the media's accepted ideal. Anything that falls outside that framework is labeled evil and deemed something that must be challenged. Upon closer examination, a democracy is defined as supreme rule via majority with no compliance to the protection of the rights of the minority from the will of the majority. These facts are cleverly hidden via government and media manipulation. Debates on the merits of democracy are usually shortened with a "greater good" that can only be established by a majority vote.

IV

Public Education

Public education is deemed necessary to compensate those who cannot afford it otherwise. As the practicality and affordability of private education or home schooling dwindle, the government grows its inroads to indoctrinate the youth.

The U.S. Department of Education (DOE) has a whopping $497.1 billion budget for the year 2021. That's a half-trillion dollars, or 4.1% of U.S. federal budgetary resources.[15]

The Department of Education's mission is as follows: ED's mission is to promote student achievement and preparation for global competitiveness by fostering educational excellence and ensuring equal access.[16]

Educational excellence?

Academic scores in reading, writing, and arithmetic have been steadily declining throughout my lifetime. To compound the problem, people actually believe they are smarter. Most people categorize themselves educationally. There are more "college-educated" people today than ever before. Degrees are being handed out like candy – very expensive candy! According to a 2017 article by Reid Wilson, just over one-third of Americans aged 25 and older hold a four-year college degree. The number of four-year

---

[15] Department of Education | Spending Profile | USAspending
[16] Mission (ed.gov)

degrees from the Census Bureau is 33.4%, and when the bureau started keeping records in 1940, that number was 4.6%.[17] Ironically, college education often adds decades of debt often without the counterbalance of exceptional incomes.

It takes the average student debt holder 19.7 years to repay their loans. America's current (2022) college student loan debt is $1.73 trillion, and this is spread out to 44.7 million people with an average monthly payment of $393.[18]

Do we have a lot of bright or educated people walking around?

Only 60 percent of all U.S. students knew that World War I was fought sometime between 1900 and 1950.

Even more shocking were the results of a survey of Oklahoma high school students conducted back in 2009. The following is a list of the questions that were asked and the percentage of students that answered correctly:

What is the supreme law of the land? ***28 percent***

What do we call the first ten amendments to the Constitution? ***26 percent***

What are the two parts of the U.S. Congress? ***27 percent***

How many justices are there on the Supreme Court? ***10 percent***

---

[17] Census: More Americans have college degrees than ever before | TheHill

[18] Average Student Loan Debt in the U.S. - 2022 Statistics | Nitro (nitrocollege.com)

Who wrote the Declaration of Independence? **14 percent**

What ocean is on the east coast of the United States? **61 percent**

What are the two major political parties in the United States? **43 percent**

We elect a U.S. senator for how many years? **11 percent**

Who was the first President of the United States? **23 percent**

Who is in charge of the executive branch? **29 percent**[19]

Unfortunately, answers like these are not unique to Oklahoma or any other state. Notice the dazed look of a cashier when the computer stalls. The basic math calculations that were just as fast as the computer during my childhood have seemingly vanished.

From the film *Truth & Lies in American Education*:

"Government schools are creating socialists and communists out of America's children with your tax dollars as they pigeonhole children into jobs to fill industry demands and call it education. American education has been stolen from parents and local communities and turned over to big government and corporate America."[20]

It is not uncommon for a child to show boredom or daydream during class. Some people believe this is because

---

[19] How Stupid Are American High School Students? – The Truth (thetruthwins.com)

[20] Truth and Lies in American Education Documentary | Indiegogo

the child subconsciously rejects the value of the subject matter. A blanket educational curriculum does not tap into all students' potential. Each child has at least a slight difference in educational taste. Autodidacticism seems to be running parallel with the Internet explosion.

Many bright and accomplished people have a peculiarity that belies formal education. Self-taught individuals surely have one big advantage – they don't operate under peer pressure. An autodidact's second advantage is that he tends to pursue his passion. His standard for excellence is different from others because he doesn't have one. His goal is to learn, and he always does. Meanwhile, most of the educational system involves memory and regurgitation rather than critical thinking, and the mass perception of a successful life is largely predicated on mastering modern education. Financial wealth as a measure of success is materialism. Pleasure can be bought. Happiness is contentment.

Tools for self-learning are available like never before. The Internet is like a library at your fingertips. An autodidact is a dictator's worst enemy.

V

Tiptoeing Through A Minefield

The Civil Rights Act of 1964 stands as a major turning point in American history, marking a decisive legal end to segregation and discrimination based on race, color, religion, sex, or national origin.[21]

Of course, there is overwhelming agreement that everyone of every race is entitled to civil rights. Discussions that start with civil rights quite often morph into arguments about which race has an unfair economic or social advantage. Public discussions about race or sex usually have parameters due to the Orwellian interjection of the catchphrase "political correctness." The latter means that genetic or cultural differences are not supposed to be considered as a primary factor of societal outcomes. Behavioral differences among races, be they genetic or environmental, are treated with kid gloves.

Most of the popular media has been in race-sensitivity overload for the past six decades, to the point where the media has even pressured legislators to take action. Public and even private discussions about race are often reviewed to find even a hint of offensiveness. This nation's most powerful people quite often speak in pre-rehearsed sentences when discussing race. Any discussion outside of an often-vague narrative can lead to a quick media verdict of racist. The racist label can be extremely burdensome. In political

---

[21] Unveiling Equality: The Civil Rights Act of 1964 - A Defining Moment in US History

circles, an established racist means one has leprosy. Even whole nations, as if that's even possible, have been deemed guilty of racism.

Confused liberals are at the forefront of today's racial and ethnic issues. Among the highest goals of the modern-day liberal is the achievement of diversity and multiculturalism. No voice has proclaimed more or louder about there being no difference among the races than modern lefties. We hear it every day – "We are all the same." These same liberals then support a plethora of Black, Hispanic, and other race-based organizations. So numerous are these orgs that listing all of them here would be impossible. However, if we were truly all the same, how would it be possible for these organizations to even exist?

Why the hyper-focus on race? Today's tyrants can use race division as a way to hang on to power. Divide-and-conquer strategies are as old as man's beginnings. Almost every story of alleged racism creates some emotional division, even in the absence of validity – elementary sociology. Many debates occur over whether a person was rightly denied something due to merit or race; however, if there is a quality instigator, there will often be hostile feelings by both parties involved. The legacy media have served as the number one instigator.

The media clearly has an infatuation with races and disparities. How often is it cited that Blacks and Hispanics have less wealth per capita than Whites? How often is it cited that the U.S. criminal justice system works in favor of Whites? The logical conclusion, especially among the non-Whites, is that there is a systemic advantage for White people. Conveniently absent from the alleged systematic bias favoring White people are statistics that demonstrate Asian-Americans have a higher average wealth level and far lower arrest rates than do Whites. The latter does not jibe with a pro-White society. Average incomes for Asian households in America are about 30% higher than incomes for Whites.[22] Of the arrests made in the U.S., 1.3% are Asian.[23] The Asian population in the U.S. is 7.2%.[24] However, Whites bias is not exonerated, at least not by the media. If the reader is surprised by this irritable contradiction, it is because these facts are very rarely discussed anywhere else.

There is, of course, good and bad in all people, and most people get along. Of course, the media continues in their quest to create infighting, especially among different races and ethnicities. Juneteenth is a federal holiday, which was signed into legislation by Joe Biden in 2021.[25]

Slavery is used as an undeniable negative, and rightly so. However, many key points are left out so as to only create racial tension. Slavery is used in the past tense, when in fact it exists today. Herewith:

"At this present moment, there are more people suffering under slavery than at any other time in history. The Global Slavery Index (GSI) estimates that more than 50

---

[22] Income By Race: Why Is Asian Income So High? - Financial Samurai
[23] Arrests And Crime Victims By Race And Ethnicity | Crime in America.Net
[24] Race Statistics in the US 2025 | Race Percentage in US – The Global Statistics
[25] Juneteenth | Federal Holiday, Meaning, Flag, History, Food, & Celebration | Britannica

million people are currently trapped in modern-day slavery."[26]

"About 150 years after most countries banned slavery – Brazil was the last to abolish its participation in the transatlantic slave trade, in 1888 – millions of men, women and children are still enslaved. Contemporary slavery takes many forms, from women forced into prostitution, to child slavery in agriculture supply chains or whole families working for nothing to pay off generational debts. Slavery thrives on every continent and in almost every country. Forced labour, people trafficking, debt bondage and child marriage are all forms of modern-day slavery that affect the world's most vulnerable people."[27]

Slavery in today's Africa and elsewhere is truly sickening. Children are preferred and kidnapped as slaves because they are less rebellious and likely to accept adult authority. Some are sold into the sex trade. All of this slavery exists even in the presence of laws against it. [28] The media and the United Nations sit silent while modern slavery thrives.

Rather than working on eradicating the considerable world slavery, the media discusses various ways to help slavery victims of the past. Another word the media parrots is reparations. As if a just system should punish children for the alleged wrongdoings of their parents, grandparents, or ancestors. The idea behind reparations may just be to create

---

[26] What is Modern Day Slavery? – voices4freedom
[27] Modern-day slavery: an explainer – Globalmarch
[28] Bing Videos

animosity on the part of Whites all the while reminding Blacks how they are behind the eight ball. Racial tension.

Multiculturalism, as in forced integration, is not the highest standard that liberals pretend it is. Multiculturalism is another vehicle for racial tension. Mutual respect while maintaining one's own values is the peaceful reconciliation to accommodate everybody. Otherwise, multiculturalism is a friction-based society.

The push for infighting is not limited to racial conflicts. My grandfather raised twelve children on his income alone, and the U.S. had a balanced budget. He worked a blue-collar factory job. Large families with single incomes were common during most of the twentieth century. Most families today have dual incomes[29], and today's budget deficit is a metaphorical ticking time bomb.[30] Is it a stretch to suggest that the government invests in pushing women into the workforce?

Chasing women into the workforce serves a trilateral purpose. It fuels unhealthy competition, grows the government financially, and allows outsiders to overinfluence children. Women are reminded that they are underappreciated in the labor force, and many will strive to change this.

The splintering has grown even more in recent years. In today's society, sexuality is used for compartmentalization.

---

[29] 53% of U.S. Households Are Dual Income - MagnifyMoney
[30] U.S. National Debt Clock : Real Time

Throughout my youth, sexual practices were mostly kept private. There was the occasional moron bragging about how he "only has four kids that he knows of," which means this man could have a child who is without necessities or being seriously harmed without the protection of a father, and he is bragging about it. There was some trivial gossip from time to time, also, but that is somewhat normal. Most people simply did not feel compelled to promote their sexuality as they do today. Even today, most people do not care who or if their neighbor has an affair with, unless it involves children or rape. Yet the media embarks on an around-the-clock campaign to promote sex as though it is a competition of sorts.

Does Hollywood create culture, or does culture create Hollywood?

My undergrad program featured an elective college class called *The American Experience Since 1945*; the class teams were assigned to give presentations of popular movies from three decades: the 1950s, 1960s, and 1970s. The speed of devolutionary morals in Hollywood was surprising. The three movies my team selected were *African Queen*, *Charade*, and *Saturday Night Fever*. In the first movie, the only skin shown on the woman was her hands and face. The second movie featured a woman in a mini skirt, and watched a hotel room door shut, implying the couple had slept together. The third movie showed teenagers having sex in their car in a parking lot. That's Hollywood brazenly attempting to modify culture to an unhealthy standard.

Today's Hollywood is infested with every kind of sexual deviant that exists. Again, most people are accepting of individuals when it comes to choosing partners. Anything from abstinence to promiscuity is considered personal. Heterosexuals make up the majority, but most people hold no animosity toward gays. The overpromotion of sexual orientation is what many people reject.

Known heretofore as a sickness, gender identity is presently promoted as fitting by the media and a significant number of government officials. Gender identity and sexual orientation diversity classroom curricula are being negotiated by organizations such as the *American Psychological Association* (APA).[31] As is the liberal playbook, they work their indoctrination at the earliest age possible, and they work it as though the subject of gender identity is even debatable.

The lack of television exposure on the international child-trafficking industry belies its reality. Today's media and governments are suspiciously reticent when it comes to discussing the estimated 244,000 to 325,000 children at risk of commercial sexual exploitation in the United States.[32] While Jeffrey Epstein's list of clients gets fumbled daily, the viewer's attention stays in the past.

How many 24/7 updates were there during the alleged pandemic of 2020? Up-to-the-minute updates are available for every election, sports scores, weather, and the stock market. There is no media campaign to update the number of children who are trafficked in the United States or around the world. How many legislators push for such a campaign?

---

[31] Sexual orientation and gender diversity
[32] 10 Things To Know About Child Trafficking - Collaborative to End Human Trafficking

The ugliness of today's media and government is real and in dire need of a spiritual cleansing.

VI

Is Counterfeiting Legal?

Cash itself has no value. The cash in your hand represents the value of your labor. Cash is an agreed-upon exchange for labor or assets.

A true money system would equilibrate labor and currency. Free markets do this. When the markets are strong-armed by government intervention, an imbalance occurs. As with all government policies, financial changes always happen under the guise of helping the people. Governments are initially established before they are hijacked.

The Federal Reserve is not federal as its name implies. It also has no reserves, as its name implies. The Federal Reserve is a privately owned banking institution whose true "reserves" lie in the fact that it has been granted the authority to create money out of thin air.

Counterfeit: made in imitation of something that has present value.

The Federal Reserve owners, along with the willing collaborators in government, have had the monetary system in exponential depreciation mode for more than a century.

The banking industry is a scam sheltered by its ability to deceive and exploit spending addictions. Most people do not recognize that the ones who want a counterfeit system are the counterfeiters who enable the spending addicts. Spending addicts are at both the private and public levels.

The symbiotic relationship between banking and government is undeniable. Governments at every level have grown primarily due to the lending institutions. The self-growing government has shifted its power from constitutional to bureaucratic at the federal level due to its ability to overspend. The alphabet agencies list is vast and growing. Here is a sample: FBI, CIA, DHS, DOE, DOJ, DEA, ATF, FDA, CDC, IRS, FTC, OSHA, NASA, FEMA, et al. These agencies have tremendous influence in the media as well. In a sound money system, the money supply would be capped, government agencies would receive only limited funding, and many would likely be eliminated altogether. Such a system would prevent the government from indebting its citizens and would subject all nonessential spending to far greater scrutiny.

Due to almost no media exposure and very few politicians willing to challenge the Federal Reserve System, the banks have thus far eluded mass public scrutiny. However, deficits are growing, and the only counterbalance is the depreciation of the currency. A collapse is inevitable. The bankers know they will face real pressure soon, so they are already pivoting. According to their playbook, they will attempt to present a new (albeit even worse) debt system as something of a convenience. They will likely agree to absorb some of the debt they helped create. However, if their cashless agenda progresses at all, it will face widespread public rejection and could ultimately trigger a broad reevaluation of the entire monetary system. Not what a thief wants. The question remains: How much longer can the criminal bankers claim they are creditors of money that was counterfeited to the public?

The vast majority of top-notch loan sharks could never get the kind of return on a loan that a bank can and does every day. Loan sharks front sound money, yet it is illegal. Fractional lending holds the banks to lending out ten times a given "loan." Hence, the bank is lending ten dollars for a hundred-dollar loan. The lendee must then give back ten times what the bank gave them, even before factoring in whatever interest was agreed on.

The US debt is at 37.5 trillion dollars, and about three million dollars are added every minute.[33] The math concludes: As of now, each US citizen owes the Federal Reserve Bank owners over $100,000.00 for money printed out of thin air. The only way for the government to pay that debt is by taxation via labor from the people. That's about two years of labor owed by each person in the US for counterfeit money! This amounts to slavery. The citizens of the US are slaves of the international banking industry.

Put in layman's terms, monetary concepts are not too hard to understand; however, the monetary conspiracy runs much deeper. A powerful cabal is needed to ensure banks stay in power. The cabal must network with media and government officers. Moreover, this cabal is most interested in accruing power. The more money lent, the more power the lender has over the lives of others, not just the borrower, but everybody else who uses the currency. If a country runs a deficit, its population owes its labor to the lender. So, were Lincoln, Garfield, McKinley, and Kennedy assassinated due to their non-conformance to the central banking cartel?

---

[33] U.S. National Debt Clock : Real Time

As with all deceptions, the shadow dancing of central banking is finite.

VII

Obamacare and the COVID Scare

Medical freedom is a recent conservative political campaign slogan. If anything, this is demonstrative of constitutional erosion. The idea that the media and the government control the medical industry has become rather apparent in the 21st Century. What often goes unnoticed is that doctors, nurses, medical school professors, and pharmacists have effectively become middle managers serving superiors who possess little real understanding of healthcare. In this century, the struggle for our own health appears to be less against disease itself and more against governments, compliant media, and opportunistic sycophants.

Government efforts to mandate health insurance represent yet another means of control. Universal healthcare is marketed as a way to protect the public's well-being by a government eager to play "big brother." The push to enforce medical insurance was a hallmark of the Obama administration, and the so-called Affordable Care Act amounted to yet another government intrusion into the free market. Like his predecessors, the nominal US leader from 2009 to 2017 simply kicked the debt can further down the road.

Though some people may be offended by my word choice, in 2020, the government, along with the media tie-in, intensely <u>claimed</u> a deadly, contagious virus was among us, and the only solution was an experimental vaccine. The vaccine was *free* and readily available for distribution by you-know-who, the government. The subsequent government borrowing from the Fed was unprecedented. Money was also spent to squelch dissident voices, labelling thousands of experienced doctors and scientists as conspiracy theorists. Ad hominem par excellence.

Being branded as a conspiracy theorist is not the biggest fear for American doctors. Doctors, nurses, medical professionals, and servicemen and women lost jobs for refusing what they considered a bioweapon. Even with subsequent court action, much of the damage was already done.

The timing of the COVID-19 virus suspiciously coincided with Donald Trump's 2020 re-election campaign. Trump would routinely gather football stadium capacities. The democrats seemed to play their last card to impeach Trump, so it was becoming super probable that Trump would win the election in a landslide. Enter the COVID-19 virus and the 6-feet-apart/no social gatherings recommendations by the CDC. Polls were locked down, ballots were counted under mistrustful circumstances, and the left was awarded a president seemingly in the early stages of dementia.

Worth mentioning during the Covid campaign, according to the World Health Organization, the 2020/2021 flu season saw a suspicious drop of 97% in death rates in the US.[34]

Never to waste a successful psychological operation, the government proceeded to push an experimental vaccine. The media and government promoted the vaccine jab as a

---

[34] Flu Has Disappeared for More Than a Year | Scientific American

lifesaver; however, a large part of the population from every demographic opposed the jab. Game on.

The subsequent battle was ugly. Friends, relatives, co-workers, neighbors, and even spouses often took sides against one another. The government and legacy media pimped the vaccine while thousands of formerly well-respected professionals warned against it. People lost jobs for refusing. In November of 2021, as an emergency temporary standard, the Occupational Safety and Health Association (OSHA) instituted an emergency policy for employers of over 100 employees to have their workers get vaccinated, or wear masks and undergo regular Covid testing by January of 2022. This mandate was upheld by the courts pending a verdict from the Supreme Court.[35]

The Supreme Court voted 6-3 against the mandate. The Supreme Court did allow the implementation of the vaccine mandate for health care workers in some federally funded facilities.[36]

The Supreme Court essentially voted against a massive rebellion and US economic collapse. That is surely what would have happened if OSHA's mandates were upheld. The bickering in everyday life continued between the pro and con vaccination camps. As the momentum of the virus's alleged lethality dwindled, booster jabs were no longer marketable.

The scandal continued until the Man behind the Curtain was exposed.

---

[35] R46288.32.pdf
[36] A Look at the Supreme Court Ruling on Vaccination Mandates - Legal Aggregate - Stanford Law School

Profiters of today's medical system are those who have the ability to deceive rather liberally. Most American adults use prescription drugs at least once a year. Drugs control symptoms; they do not cure diseases. Therefore, prescription drugs are cash cows for doctors, insurance companies, and hospitals. You are a customer, not a patient.

Hardly an hour passes on television, radio, or the Internet without an advertisement for prescription drugs. Direct-to-consumer pharmaceutical marketing bears an uncanny resemblance to a street-corner drug dealer's pitch—though with one key difference: prescription drugs come with a long list of potentially harmful side effects. Yet when someone taking multiple prescriptions dies prematurely, the cause is often attributed to "complications" from the underlying illness rather than to the drugs that may have triggered or worsened their decline.

Nothing is free. Health care companies often make on-site employer visits to perform free "lifesaving health screenings." Sounds like a bargain unless you understand these companies will soon be profiting off of the subsequent healthcare visits and prescription drugs that will not be free. Following a surreal Covid scare campaign in 2020, much of the frightened population was begging for an out. The out was a free jab on Uncle Sam's dime, sometimes given with a complimentary donut.

Notwithstanding, there are many good doctors, hospitals, and treatments that are available to the general population. Some drugs are necessary and helpful. Surgeries sometimes save lives as well. The lead-up to most health issues that will require drugs or surgery is repetitive and involves unwise choices. Indeed, the vast majority of health issues are the result of lifestyle. Poor diet, stress, lack of exercise, lack of sunshine, and chemical addictions are some of the most common causes of health issues. No doctor, drug, or surgery can correct these habits. Spiritual change can, and it's free.

Many rich and powerful corporations spend money on ads designed to sell their products, even at the cost of deception. The ad (low fat, sugar, carb, cholesterol, calorie, etc.) seems like a healthy choice on its face, but other ingredients are often not featured in the advertisement campaign.

Whole industries can fund research to disguise dangers that may otherwise become apparent sooner rather than later. According to the following article *50 Years Ago, Sugar Industry Quietly Paid Scientists To Point Blame At Fat*, scientists ignored documented research on the dangers of sugar consumption. In the 1950s, there was already research demonstrating a link between heart disease and sugar consumption: The article draws on internal documents to show that an industry group called the Sugar Research Foundation wanted to "refute" concerns about sugar's possible role in heart disease. The SRF then sponsored research by Harvard scientists that did just that. The result was published in the *New England Journal of Medicine* in 1967, with no disclosure of the sugar industry funding.[37]

---

[37] 50 Years Ago, Sugar Industry Quietly Paid Scientists To Point Blame At Fat : The Two-Way : NPR

I remember in the 1980s reading and hearing about heart disease being the number one killer for men. My young adulthood harbored a fascination for health and fitness. The more I educated myself, the more I understood the importance of rest, exercise, and nutrition. Of the three, nutrition would receive the most attention, and sales were the likely culprit. Food labels always started out with calories, overall fat, and saturated fat content, and sugar was listed in total grams, but not openly correlated with overall calories. The bias was in, and the primary purpose of a food label appeared to be moderating fat consumption. The following decades have seen a significant spike in diabetes and cancer, even with all the saturated fat warnings. Sugar consumption was about 4 pounds annually per person in the year 1700. Today, 50% of Americans eat 180 pounds of sugar per year.[38]

All the while, Americans were gaining weight beyond healthy levels, and the sugar industry cashed in. Sugar creates spikes in energy but has empty calories. The latter means that these calories have almost no nutritional value, i.e., vitamins, minerals, or fiber. Foods with loads of sugar were being touted as "fat-free." A 12-ounce can of popular sodas has approximately 10 teaspoons of sugar in it, and in a 2015 study, there were 184,000 deaths attributed to sweetened beverages.[39]

When you have industries capable of tampering with science, should you always "trust the science?"

---

[38] Sugar: "The White Death" (believespecialtyshop.ca)
[39] How Much Sugar Is in Soda? | POPSUGAR Fitness

A la the government, the health industry is surreptitiously expanding. Super-expensive agencies regulate food and drugs for consumption. Our grocery stores are loaded with junk food. Our health care providers prescribe billions of prescriptions each year. The consumers are paying for chemicals rather than food and medicine. American women, on average, weigh as much as American men did 60 years ago.[40]

In an ideal society, doctors who had healthy patients would be paid the most.

I am a medical autodidact rather than a medical professional. With the bloated profits in the industry and its link to the government, I choose to stay that way.

---

[40] Average US Woman Weighs What a Man Did in 1960s - Tufts Health & Nutrition Letter

VIII

Organized Religion or Spiritual Control

I wish to preface this chapter by first saying that I understand how important each person's faith is. However, more attention must be paid to every aspect of our social structure to escape external control and rediscover our intelligence. The organizers of religions are unexposed, yet have substantial influence on the behavior of their huge congregations.

We are spiritual beings in a physical body. Proof exists that body and spirit are separate. This is why amputees remain 100% mindfully and soulfully intact. Spirituality is also not the same as religion. At some point, an authoritative class formally established a belief system with a hierarchical structure, aka organized religion. The system was institutionalized and splintered.

Inquisitiveness yields dividends. Skeptics of organized religion do not wish to change the many good practices learned by millions of religious followers; however, due to the absence of tangible evidence, religion creates many questions. Is questioning organized religion a distrust in God or man?

The following questions can be asked of organized religion:

Why does God hide his presence and relay his thoughts through somebody else? Why shouldn't all books, even religious ones, allow for some cross-examination? If I am not supposed to question God, why did He make me so inquisitive? Why did the all-powerful, all-knowing, and all-loving God create a perennial sinner and then beat him over the head for all of eternity? Why is there a forever heaven-or-hell punishment awaiting everybody after death, with no modification to adjust for a fairer karmic judgment? *Why would God ever trust a criminal priest or bishop? Why would God have to put his words in print?* How many people leave churches every day with guilt, fear, shame, and gaslit? How many others leave to enter their communities as virtue signalers looking for prey? Why is organized religion as a whole disjointed? Can man corrupt religions? *Is God a noun or a verb, internal or external? Could God just mean good with just one o? Could the devil mean evil with an added d?*

Few topics stir emotions as deeply as religion. For many, it takes precedence over everything else in life, even friends and family. To merely question or highlight the implausibility of stories from a sacred text is to cross a line in the eyes of the believer. From an epistemological standpoint, religions are ultimately opinions, yet their followers place extraordinary weight on what is, at its core, a supposition.

Isn't the word believe a singular oxymoron? You cannot make somebody believe something; the effort is about control. Nor can you force yourself to believe things; you can accept the possibility. Even the most strident believers latently acknowledge this. The acknowledgment comes in the form of unprovability. When something, anything, is unprovable, it is said to be believed or not believed. How provable is religion? Suffice it to say that the provable aspects of religion are its incomprehensibility.

So, who serves as the overseer when it comes to religion? Most people believe that the overseer is God, with sacred texts and preachers acting under divine inspiration. Those who question this framework are often labeled "agnostic"—a term that simply denotes acceptance of not knowing. Agnostics are not confused; rather, they acknowledge uncertainty. Yet they are frequently mistaken for atheists, or deliberately conflated with them, as if both positions were inherently opposed to God.

To add to the friction, the agnostics see religious zealots as perhaps living fake lives. So many people place judgments based on religion and God. Religion is a personal choice, and no one has dibs on what or who or if God is. However, there is and should be a mutual respect among people who have different or no religious beliefs.

One thing that organized religion has as a common thread is the atheism involved in each separate one. There are at least a few different religions. Using a conservative number of five different religions, each adherent rejects four out of the five. An atheist rejects all five, only one more than followers of a specific religion.

Most people do not choose their religions; they are subjects of a worldwide, disjointed, organized religious empire. I started my life as a Catholic. How many religious folks actually chose their religion? We didn't. The choice was made by our parents, and our parents by theirs, and so on. As a young child, my church attendance was mandated by my parents as well as the Catholic schools I attended. As most other followers of organized religions do, I felt a sense of moral superiority. In reality, the majority of people in America's prisons are religiously affiliated. In a study of state penitentiaries, two-thirds of the inmates were Christians.[41] So, why the disconnect between religion and behavior?

Man has corrupted governments, education, media, corporations, banking, health care, and even charities (no citation needed for any of these). Hence, it definitely stands to reason that man can corrupt organized religion.

More conspiracies are examined in the world today than ever before. For a conspiracy to be examined, there must be a seed of merit to it. Governments and popular media outlets have been scrutinized relentlessly due to the consistency of their inconsistencies. I digress; the US Constitution is a document of convenience.

Most people today recognize that corruption is rampant in politics and the media, and merely debate how deep it runs. What often escapes similar scrutiny, however, is organized religion. Despite the scientific implausibility of many religious claims, the majority of adherents still regard blasphemy as an outrageously serious offense. Perhaps blasphemy is a feature of organized religion for that reason. Hijacking of governments, media, corporations, and banks is

---

[41] Chaplains' Perspectives on the Religious Lives of Inmates | Pew Research Center

relatively easy to prove and accept; hijacking of religions is extremely hard for many to accept. To prove church shenanigans, the parishioners must let their guard down. A guard that has become second nature via decades of religious practice.

The God in organized religions seems to possess an overabundance of arrogance. God is an all-powerful, perfect entity; do what He says, hit your knees, bow your head, and exclaim You are not worthy to receive Him. You'd better do this every day throughout your life. In all honesty, this sounds like an insecure bully.

The supposed separation of church and state is largely an illusion. In practice, churches function under government oversight, even in countries with a single dominant religion. Governments are the ultimate arbiters, determining whether and how organized religions may operate within their borders. Since no land on Earth exists outside governmental control, it follows that, by human law, government authority supersedes all organized religions.

Interpreting God's law is the job of the seller. The sale begins by preaching His benevolence. There is a confirmation bias among those who preach religion. Fluctuations in luck are a great example. When unexpected good fortune happens, a given God is the recipient of the credit. Conversely, when an unfortunate accident happens, it may be considered a learning experience, but it is never blamed on that same God, even though He had the power to stop it. Even stating this causes a cringe moment for some. The fact that there is a guilt complex even among honest critics of organized religion gives testament to the fact that sensitivity has occurred from years of religious brainwashing.

All religious followers acknowledge that they believe in something they cannot provide tangible evidence for. Imagine a religious professional who is employed as a psychiatrist. He examines one of his patients and discovers that this patient has an imaginary friend and has daily back-and-forth conversations with him. The psychiatrist may then diagnose the patient with some type of dissociative disorder and recommend drugs, follow-ups, or even institutionalization to help get over his illness. In the face of this, the psychiatrist leaves his office, then visits his place of worship and has his own conversation with someone who is not there either. Another cringe moment.

Organized religions all come with a carefully orchestrated fear campaign. If you don't follow the rules, you will suffer for eternity. Many religions state that money is the root of all evil, then pressure followers for monetary contributions in the next breath. Whilst researching religion, I stumbled across an interesting word, tithe, which means budgeted financial support of a church, like a tax.

"Tithing is a practice that has been taught and emphasized in many churches for centuries. Yet, despite its prominence, some Christians still struggle to embrace this financial principle. However, what many people fail to realize is that the consequences of not tithing are far more significant than they might think. In this article, we will explore the harsh realities of a non-tither and what it truly means to neglect this critical principle."[42]

The blog cited above goes on to explain that the non-tither does not trust God, lives under a curse, and is a robber. The non-tither has moved against God, who has the power to punish him with hell for all of eternity. This is extortion, which is illegal everywhere else. Religious exemption par excellence!

A primary feature of organized religion is the wonderment of believing without the need for sensory verification. Quasi-factualization. For you to believe something, the purveyor of such does not need any proof of its existence. Relieving someone of that responsibility gives them corruptibility. Manipulation occurs when religious leaders (authoritarians?) promote the idea that there is punishment for those who do not abandon their original senses in favor of what they are told, i.e., let go absolutely.

Haven't there been instances where a religious representative does something to contradict the very principles of his religion? His next move is swift and predictable. He, of course, confesses his offense and is given forgiveness because he is "truly sorry." Most adults have figured out that being truly sorry will or will not be demonstrated in future actions. Nonetheless, when the penance is complete, the parishioner is absolved as long as he agrees to follow the religious authority.

Questioning man's interpretation of God is a delicately accepted concept. Playing the role of impartial, if there were

---

[42] 5 Truths About Non-Tithers

an all-powerful God as most religions profess, there would not be a need for organized religion per se. If, on the other hand, there was no all-powerful God, then organized religion would be a formidable methodology of control. Not the least of which would be the people's reluctance to revolt against the will of God.

The human element within church hierarchies undoubtedly interferes with religious popularity. Among the followers of Catholicism, ugliness is exponentially exacerbated when a priest, bishop, cardinal, or pope commits a flagrant sin. These are clearly humans acting independently of any benevolent God. Yet before the sin, how many times have these religious representatives successfully played the "Holier than thou card?" Religion has a lot to do with trust. The parishioner trusts that God's conduit is a legitimate guide. Most parishioners will not abandon their faith even if the trust is breached. The churchgoer holds on to the doctrine and either forgives the offense or readily accepts a new conduit. How much of this readiness to keep believing has to do with the fear of death and subsequent afterlife placement?

Upon death, a family will usually organize a funeral to honor the life of the deceased person. The overwhelming majority of these ceremonies could be classified as religious advertisements. The day is spent with the friends and relatives of the deceased, with the primary focus on the link between the afterlife of the person and his or her religious connection. Having control of everybody's afterlife would certainly place God above any other authority. However, if man has that illusory power, he has significant control over the lives of his contemporaries.

Something I naturally question is the pope's purported ability to canonize people for "Official" sainthood. Playing devil's advocate – no pun intended – and assuming all of these people led pure lives, would there not be non-Christians deserving of saintly status as well? A code of correct morals does not translate into an authoritative hierarchy.

The agnostic, or questioner, does not dismiss the good values found in most organized religions. The seven deadly sins or capital vices are excellent examples of how not to act. The seven heavenly virtues play the role of spoilers to these. The most popular book ever written is the Holy Bible; whether you agree with it verbatim or not, the book commands respect. The Bible also offers metaphors for those who are spiritual but not religious. Many of those who cite the Bible, religious or not, will accept interpreted views from it.

It seems like, at some point, there was an evolution from spirituality, the original religion, to organized religion. Could there be another form of organized religion not being defined as such? Governments all over the supposedly free nations are encroaching on the expression of personal opinions. The government officials, along with their inroads into the media, are preaching what is and is not moral. For sure. Moreover, they seem to be/are dictating what is sacred.

There are laws in many countries that force citizens to accept *ideological verities*. Dissident opinion may result in civil and or criminal punishment. Does this not sound like organized religion? The doctrine is accepted even with some private disagreement.

Holding a personal view of God is unacceptable within organized religion; only adherence to doctrine and its hierarchical interpretation is permitted. Likewise, how many governments genuinely function as republics or representative bodies? The answer is none, for to govern, by its very definition, is to control, not to serve the governed.

Just like organized religion, one is born into one's country. The parents and educational system explain the dos and don'ts. The person grows to acquaint and acquiesce. In adulthood, the person then explains the rules to the youth. An example of government being religious is its disapproval of dissent. Criticizing wars, even in the good ole USA, is often viewed as somewhere between unpatriotic and treasonous.

The following is from the Bible's Romans 13: Let everyone be subject to the governing authorities, for there is no authority except that which God has established. The authorities that exist have been established by God.

[2] Consequently, whoever rebels against the authority is rebelling against what God has instituted, and those who do so will bring judgment on themselves.

[3] For rulers hold no terror for those who do right, but for those who do wrong. Do you want to be free from fear of the one in authority? Then do what is right and you will be commended.

⁴ For the one in authority is God's servant for your good. But if you do wrong, be afraid, for rulers do not bear the sword for no reason. They are God's servants, agents of wrath to bring punishment on the wrongdoer.

⁵ Therefore, it is necessary to submit to the authorities, not only because of possible punishment but also as a matter of conscience.

⁶ This is also why you pay taxes, for the authorities are God's servants, who give their full time to governing. ⁷ Give to everyone what you owe them: If you owe taxes, pay taxes; if revenue, then revenue; if respect, then respect; if honor, then honor.

I was not around to witness who wrote or edited the Bible, but judging by the preponderance of evidence, the above verses clearly suggest the work of Earthly authoritarians.

Is there any tangible evidence of Christ's existence here on Earth? Christians claim Jesus Christ walked the Earth and was the Son of God the Father. There are some reasonable questions as to the extent of Jesus Christ's suffering and sacrifice, however. Christ himself was said to have "given his life" for the sins of mankind. Accordingly, he suffered and then died on Good Friday and rose from the dead two days later on Easter Sunday. This means what he gave up was only two days of life for mankind's sins. Some religions run contrary to the literal stories of Christ's life, claiming that Christ consciousness is within us all. With Christ Consciousness, we may connect to the divine spark within us. "The kingdom of God is within you. They've been hiding this from you for 2,000 years. Because a soul that remembers it's divine is a soul that cannot be controlled."[43]

IX

The Father of Lies

People see the world through the lens of their own morality and level of boldness. White lies generally fall within the parameters of acceptable behavior.

The 40 Lies Everyone Tells on a Daily Basis is an interesting and quick read that I believe most people can relate to. I whittled this list down to a dozen:

My phone has been acting weird

Let's just do one more

I don't really watch TV

I'm almost finished

I read/watched that a while ago

That makes sense

Oh shoot, I forgot to do that

Traffic was nuts

That's interesting

I gotta run

I've been totally slammed

This is delicious!

Article and list from Alex Daniel.[44]

In reality, it is unconsciously assumed that people exaggerate. Big lies, on the other hand, are unconscionable. It is assumed that people would never tell a life-altering lie.

Assuming the reader does not have a knee-jerk reaction brought on by the author cited, the text of this argument makes a lot of sense: from Adolph Hitler's *Mein Kampf* (1925):

"All this was inspired by the principle—which is quite true within itself—that in the big lie there is always a certain force of credibility; because the broad masses of a nation are always more easily corrupted in the deeper strata of their emotional nature than consciously or voluntarily; and thus in the primitive simplicity of their minds they more readily fall victims to the big lie than the small lie, since they themselves often tell small lies in little matters but would be ashamed to resort to large-scale falsehoods.

It would never come into their heads to fabricate colossal untruths, and they would not believe that others could have the impudence to distort the truth so infamously. Even though the facts which prove this to be so may be brought clearly to their minds, they will still doubt and waver and will continue to think that there may be some other explanation. For the grossly impudent lie always leaves traces behind it, even after it has been nailed down, a fact

---

[44] The 40 Common White Lies Everyone Tells on a Daily Basis — Best Life (bestlifeonline.com)

which is known to all expert liars in this world and to all who conspire together in the art of lying."[45]

---

[45]The Big Lie – Propaganda Principle #1 (dailykos.com)

PROCEED

WITH

CAUTION

"You take the blue pill... the story ends, you wake up in your bed and believe whatever you want to believe. You take the red pill... you stay in <u>Wonderland</u>, and I show you how deep the rabbit hole goes."

A growing share of the population now recognizes that the media and the government are not on their side—the illusion is fading. The COVID episode may well have been the final straw, though perhaps the public would have awakened eventually. Wars continue, debt keeps climbing, and alternative information sources have become more reliable and widespread. Even religious leaders are facing increased scrutiny. For those willing to delve deeper down the rabbit hole, the discoveries awaiting them could expose and potentially unravel the entire corrupt control matrix that shapes our world.

A flat, stationary Earth cannot co-exist with the present system!

The present system is more invested in a spinning spherical Earth than it is in the rapidly depreciating dollar. The media also survives in a depreciating state. And even with a "lesser of two evils" choice and a gerrymandered election process, voting rights keep the hope of a better government alive. Now prove the Earth is flat, and watch those dominoes all fall.

One plus one is two. If the latter is false, all subsequent math equations will be wrong. If the Earth is flat, elementary education is wrong. If elementary education is wrong, then higher education has no foundation.

Mandatory education states that the Earth is a spinning ball occupying less than a septillionth of the size of the rest of space. Your senses tell you that you are not spinning at over 1,000 miles per hour, but the government and your television tell you that you are.

Pandora's Ball

A simple cosmology has reemerged from its long-lost vibrancy.

People must be taught from a very young age, graded on their compliance, ridiculed for questioning, and constantly reminded throughout their lives that they live on a massive sphere spinning at supersonic speed while orbiting the sun even faster—because without such an intense and continuous campaign, the idea would never make it past third grade.

Performing a Google search typing the words "Flat Earth theory" produces a first page of non-seriousness, as though the concept itself is somewhere between a joke and full-blown craziness. The globe Earth model was impregnable during the decades before the proliferation of flat-Earth theory on the Internet. Some currently say we have a motionless Earth, flat, level, and circular, but not spherical. No planetoid spheres above us. The sun, moon, and all stars except Polaris rotate. These arguments weren't hard to ignore a couple of decades ago because they only existed at inconsequential levels. *The times (they) are a-changing.*[46]

Flat Earth piqued my interest circa 2015. Once I accepted the Earth could be flat as a viable concept, I did what I was taught as a researcher. Critical thinking requires demanding two opposing perspectives for full transparency. I quickly discovered that the best the heliocentric Earth model could do was appeal to authority, confirmation bias,

---

[46] Times are changing - Idioms by The Free Dictionary

bandwagon, strawman, and other fallacies. The geocentric model gained pole position (no pun intended) as the far more reasonable theory.

Interestingly enough, flat-Earthers know more about what most people believe than the believers do! The average person is simply okay with whatever is written in science books and shown on television. Most never truly study the supposed motion speeds, measurements, or curvature calculations. The Earth supposedly spins at 1,037mph, revolves around the sun at 67,000mph, is 25,000 miles in circumference, and curves in all directions at 8 inches per mile squared, and most people don't know it – they don't even know what they "believe." Flat-Earthers know all of these purported scientific *facts*.

Our senses corroborate a flat and stationary Earth. If the Earth were spinning once per day (1,037mph) and revolving around the sun once per year (67,000mph), how is the North Star always in the same place during every night sky?

Is the tangled web woven by the heliocentric dynasty destined to become a feature of future history books?

I

Fallacies

One way to broaden your support base is to use facts and figures misleadingly.

"There's a world of difference between truth and facts. Facts can obscure the truth." – Maya Angelou.[47]

It seems as though every time during those rare times that flat Earthers are accepted into a debate, there is an overreliance on fallacies.

The bandwagon fallacy sits at the front of every globe vs. flat-Earth debate. The overwhelming majority of people not only believe the Earth is a spinning sphere, but they also don't even consider an alternate view. Even though popularity has no actual impact on whether something is true, people tend to follow the crowd.

An appeal to authority argument is often the quickest way to silence a flat-Earther. After all, it's hard to believe that scientists, physicists, astronauts, and great minds like Pythagoras, Aristotle, Galileo, Newton, Einstein, and countless others, not to mention world leaders, could all be wrong.

Personal incredulity. Many people simply don't understand how the Earth could be flat. They don't understand it because they never investigated it. There is comfort in believing that our educational system is always

---

[47] Maya Angelou: 'There's a world of difference between truth and facts. Facts can obscure the truth.' — The Socratic Method

correct, and the designers would not steer people in the wrong direction. They also don't understand what anybody would have to gain to hide the Earth's true shape. Moreover, they don't understand how a group of insiders could pull off such an incredible worldwide lie.

The strawman fallacy occurs when someone misrepresents an opponent's argument to make it easier to attack. For example, critics sometimes claim that flat-Earthers believe you can sail far enough across the ocean and "fall off the edge." This is inaccurate. Flat-Earthers typically hold that the Earth is a disk surrounded by an ice wall, identified as Antarctica, rather than having any literal edge.

The red herring fallacy is used to distract from the main issue. When challenged to provide evidence of the Earth's curvature, a key feature if the planet were truly spherical, flat-Earth proponents argue that no one has ever demonstrated such curvature. In response, their opponents often deflect by questioning why anyone would reject "established science," rather than addressing the claim directly.

All flat-Earthers run into the ad hominem fallacy. This fallacy steers away from the argument itself and directs attention toward the character of the debater instead. This tactic often follows a point in the debate that cannot be rejected on merit.

II

Mathematics

Math is the antecedent of scientific facts. Because most people recognize the value of math when making a scientific claim, those who claim the Earth is a spinning ball always include a plethora of mathematical jargon. For most people, the encoded complexities make the decoding not worthwhile. The latter is the primary reason why flat-Earthers (geocentric) know more about what spinning-ball-Earthers (heliocentric) believe about spinning-ball-Earth than those who believe it do.

To prove whether the Earth is a flat plane or a spheroid, there has to be a starting point in a mathematical equation. The starting point of the globe-Earth model is that the Earth is a spheroid, 24,859 miles in circumference and 7,918 miles in diameter.[48]

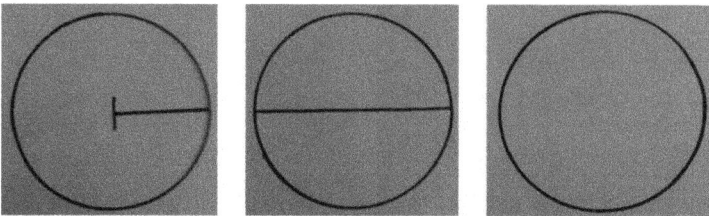

Radius = 3,959 miles

Diameter = 7,918 miles

---

[48] Earth - Wikipedia

Circumference = 24,859 miles

When performing calculations on a spheroid, it is important to note that it has curvature in every direction. According to the overall size of the spheroid, certain calculations will apply. The spherical trigonometry adjusted for the calculations above is 8 inches of the downward curve for the square of each mile from two points. In other words:

1 mile = 8 inches

2 miles = 2 x 2 = 4 x 8 inches = 2 feet, 8 inches

3 miles = 3 x 3 = 9 x 8 inches = 6 feet

10 miles = 10 x 10 = 100 x 8 inches = 66 feet, 8 inches

50 miles = 50 x 50 = 2,500 x 8 inches = 1,666 feet, 8 inches

100 miles = 100 x 100 = 10,000 x 8 inches = 6,666 feet, 8 inches[49]

To conclude, Math comes before science, and since most people don't understand the math behind the globe model, they just accept it without question. Flat-Earthers understand the math better, and if we actually apply it, we find that the supposed curvature of the Earth doesn't match what we see.

---

[49] Earth Curvature Calculator – FLAT EARTH BILL

III

Water

The surfaces of all standing water are level, hence sea level. Most people never ponder this fact deeply enough to realize it also makes the Earth horizontal. Since over 70% of Earth's surface is water, the only way the Earth could be a sphere would be if the lakes and oceans had a convexity to their surfaces. The current science and geography books used at every level of education claim that the Earth is a globe with a nearly 25,000-mile circumference. Using the above spherical trigonometry, if there were 3 miles between two boats, there would also be 6 feet of convexity between them, according to science texts. The surface of any body of standing water has exactly zero convexity by experiment, eyesight, lasers, telescopes, periscopes, and cameras.

Many people still believe that boats disappear over the horizon, yet fail to consider the limit of human eyesight, a vanishing point. However, when the viewer uses a zoom lens, the boat comes back into sight, and the vanishing point is pushed back several times further. The farther away something is, the smaller it becomes to our sense of sight, and at some point, it will disappear. A helium birthday balloon goes high in the sky and does not disappear due to some curve. Have you ever had somebody walking toward you from a far distance who you didn't recognize until they came into view? If they were holding a small object such as a ball, you would not be able to see it until the person walked to a close enough distance. The same is true when something moves away from you. A vanishing point is inevitable. With a strong enough telescope, you'd be able to make out your friend's face as well as what he was carrying as soon as he came into first view. This is a do-it-yourself experiment that's pretty easy.

If people would take the time to observe and test what they see, instead of accepting what they are told, they might begin to question the shape of the world beneath their feet. Science should always begin with observation, not assumption. When every lake, sea, and ocean proves itself perfectly level to our senses and instruments, perhaps it's worth asking whether the globe model describes our world, or just the one we've been taught to imagine.

IV

Skyline/Horizon

The horizon is another giveaway concerning the shape of the Earth. The alleged ball shape could only exist if the horizon corroborated it.

The Chicago skyline is visible from 50 miles away, as seen in a beautiful sunset photo on worldnewsinpictures.com.[50] Most of the comments below the article discuss the picture's beauty; however, a couple of posters mention information that contradicts globe math. At a distance of 50 miles, spherical trigonometry would dictate a horizon loss of 1,667 feet. The tallest building in the Chicago skyline is 1,450 feet, making it impossible to see from the Earth if the Earth were a globe with a diameter of 8,000 miles and a circumference of 25,000 miles. The Statue of Liberty is 326 feet tall and can be seen from a distance of 60 miles away. Using the same trigonometry calculations, the torch would be 2,074 feet below the horizon if the Earth were a ball.[51]

The horizon appears level and flat from a panoramic view. The Earth's horizon from extremely high altitudes in hot air balloons appears flat with no curve, as if it were 180 degrees. Upon ascension and throughout the trips, the horizon remains fixed/level. If the Earth were spherical, once

---

[50] Chicago Skyline Visible From Nearly 50 Miles Away In Indiana Dunes Sunset (worldnewsinpictures.com)
[51] Flat Plane Earth - 200 Proofs Earth is Not a Spinning Ball by Eric Dubay (rumble.com)

the horizon came into view, the passenger would have to keep tilting his head in order to see the horizon.

Whenever meteors shoot across the sky, they always appear from above and disappear at the horizon. If Earth were a huge spinning ball, meteor activity would at least sometimes start from the horizon. Or am I missing something?

V

Planes

Commercial planes fly nonstop and stay at the same altitude throughout their flights. Bringing a level on a plane makes for an excellent and easy-to-do experiment that any traveler could conduct. If the plane stayed level, so would the level. If there were continual nose-diving, the bubble inside the level would be off-center. In an article called *A Flat-Earther's Experiment Goes Viral For All The Wrong Reasons* a flat-Earther used a level on an airplane, then posted his results via a YouTube video. The level did not move for 23 minutes, so the plane was not dipping its nose to account for the several miles of curvature it would have lost if flying over a ball-Earth.[52]

On a ball-Earth, 25,000 miles in circumference, planes would be required to constantly dip their noses throughout their flights in order to maintain their altitude. At a cruising speed of 500mph, an airplane would have to descend 2,777 feet every minute in order to maintain altitude. If an airplane did not continually adjust its altitude to follow the Earth's curvature, it would supposedly rise about 31.5 miles above the surface after an hour of flight. By that logic, rockets would be unnecessary, planes that simply maintained a straight path could eventually fly right into space.

---

[52] A Flat-Earther's Experiment Goes Viral For All The Wrong Reasons - Oddee

Picture a Ferris wheel. The airport flight distance from Los Angeles to New York is 2,475 miles.[53] On a ball Earth of nearly 25,000 miles in circumference, this (L.A. to N.Y) would make up 10%, also converted to 36 degrees.

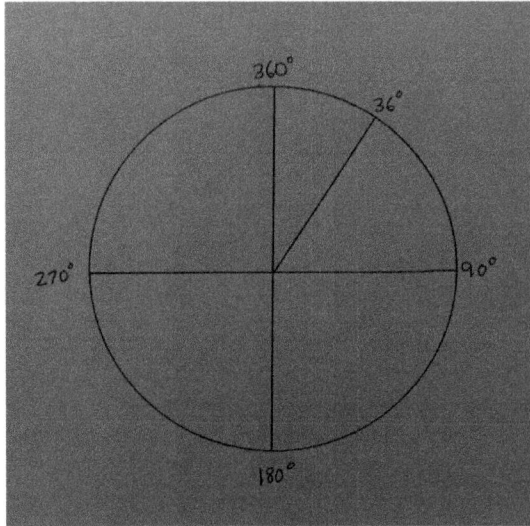

Notice the absurdity in suggesting a plane could fly 36 degrees on a ball without continual dipping along the way.

If the Earth were spinning as the current science claims it is, then planes traveling eastward and westward would have to seriously revise their ETA's due to the 1,000mph spin of the Earth, right? If a helicopter hovered overhead for 12 hours, it should come down on the other side of the spinning-ball Earth. To counter the validity of the latter, heliocentric proponents claim that the atmosphere surrounding the Earth is somehow synchronized with the

---

[53] Los Angeles to New York distance (LAX to JFK) | Air Miles Calculator

Earth, and everybody's common sense is thereby misled, a clear-cut appeal to authority fallacy.

Interestingly, but not surprisingly to flat-Earthers, pilots are among the supporters of a pro-flat and stationary Earth. Who would know more about the environment and details of a job than those who are employed to perform it every day? There would have to be visible curvature, as well as a way to account for that curvature, if the Earth were spherical. As of February 13, 2022, a Facebook page called Pilots & Friends Supporting the FE (Proven by Science and Mathematics) has 9,000 members.[54] The posts on the page routinely demonstrate the contradictions of mapping trips on a globe Earth model.

On a 2015 plane flight from Taiwan to Los Angeles, a pregnant lady went into labor, and the plane made an emergency landing in Alaska. The BBC noted a peculiarity involved. Was the controversy that the plane landed way off course in Alaska rather than Hawaii? Only on a flat Earth model is Alaska a much better choice for an emergency land, because it is directly between Taiwan and Los Angeles. The controversy explained by the BBC had to do with accusations that the woman wanted to give birth in the United States, where the child could gain citizenship rights. The nonconforming globe flight path was completely ignored in this story.[55]

As Eric Dubay mentions in his *200 Proofs Earth is Not a Spinning Ball,* many flight paths make no sense on a ball-

[54] Pilots & Friends Supporting the FE (Proven by Science and Mathematics) | Facebook
[55] Plane birth sparks controversy in Taiwan - BBC News

shaped Earth, yet perfect sense on a flat Earth. Routing from Johannesburg to Perth, Australia, with a stopover in Dubai amounts to a north-northeast trajectory on a trip that is almost directly eastward. The shortest distance between two points is a straight line.[56]

---

[56] 200 Proofs Earth is Not a Spinning Ball (HD Remastered)

VI

Junk science

Popular science has been used as a go-to argument to secure debates. Science is unashamedly promoted as a synonym for truth. Science is a subject, and truth has the power to change it.

Science, any system of knowledge that is concerned with the physical world and its phenomena and that entails unbiased observations and systematic experimentation. In general, science involves the pursuit of knowledge about general truths or the operation of fundamental laws.[57]

Science is taught to the public as being objective. When science stays in its natural form, it is objective. According to the online definition from Merriam-Webster; **objective**: expressing or dealing with facts or conditions as perceived without distortion by personal feelings, prejudices, or interpretations.[58]

On the Scientific American (Science Talk) website, there is an article called *Flat Earthers: What They Believe and Why*. The first paragraph reads: Michael Marshall, project director of the Good Thinking Society in the U.K., discusses flat-earth beliefs and their relationship to conspiracy theories and other antiscience activities.[59]

---

[57] Science | Definition, Disciplines, & Facts | Britannica
[58] Objective Definition & Meaning - Merriam-Webster
[59] Flat Earthers: What They Believe and Why - Scientific American

So much of flat-Earth theory is based on empirical evidence rather than appeals to authority.

Science does not speak with an interpretive voice. So, to make statements like "it goes against science" is a bogus argument. The subject of science is man's understanding of nature, so it is in a constant state of revision and must continually be questioned and scrutinized. As much weight as a "scientific fact" has today may be relegated to the outdated tomorrow.

Trusting the science also means trusting those who are in control of it. What that means is that the elite within our power structure have the ability to use science as a mechanism for control. So much so that they call scientific theories *scientific laws*.

In an excellent 1984 article, David Dickson contends that banking, corporate, and military control the nation's future. The chief strength of his book is a veneer of provocative ideas that will force even those familiar with American science policy to reassess conventional interpretations of recent trends. Is it possible, as he asserts, that the greater public participation in debates over genetic engineering, environmental hazards and other technical issues cherished by the "public interest" movement may actually be reducing democratic control over technology because it disguises the fact that existing power structures remain in control? Is it true that the whole technology assessment movement, which seeks to define the hazards of new technologies, is antidemocratic because it reduces political conflicts to technical terms and thus leaves technocrats rather than democrats in control? Is it conceivable that efforts to improve science teaching in the public schools are not designed to produce a more informed and questioning electorate but only "to generate a greater willingness to accept the conclusions of scientific experts"?[60]

Who are the "experts?" When an individual makes a mistake, it falls on him. When an expert makes a mistake, it hurts everyone who relies on his judgment. Experts make people comfortable and stroke their audience's lazy side. Experts are often not even questioned due to their label.

NASA employs many such experts.

The job application at NASA is 80 times harder than the one to get into Harvard. In 2017, NASA received a record 18,300 applications; 12 applicants were selected. [61]

Just like science, history is not so objective either.

Isaac Newton is purported to have an IQ of 192:

The English physicist and mathematician. He is regarded as having developed much of calculus, the building blocks of today's engineering feats. His Mathematical Principles of Natural Philosophy is one of the most influential scientific works, heralding the Age of Enlightenment, when Europe entered an era of advancements that gave birth to modern technologies.

---

[60] WHO CONTROLS SCIENCE? - The New York Times (nytimes.com)
[61] NASA's Application Is 80 Times Harder Than Getting into Harvard. The Chosen Ones Have These Skills In Common | Inc.com

Galileo is purported to have an IQ of 182:

The Italian physicist, astronomer, mathematician, and philosopher. He is best known for giving us the telescope. But that's just a mere speck in his wide-reaching scientific achievements, namely the discovery of planetary objects such as Callisto, Galilean moons, Europa, Ganymede, and Io. He was also responsible for confirming, through actual observation, the heliocentric nature of the solar system—the sun is at the center and the planets revolve around it—putting him at the crosshairs of the Inquisition during his time.[62]

According to the Mensa International website, Sir Francis Galton was the first scientist to attempt to devise a modern intelligence test. His contributions began in 1884. The two aforementioned super-geniuses were already centuries deceased by then. An average I.Q. is 100, and a score of 145 would rank an individual in the 99.9 percentile.[63] The likelihood of a 182 I.Q. is one in 43 million, and 192 is one in 2.3 billion.[64] Given the world's population during their lives of 500-600 million,[65] Galileo would have been one of the eleven or twelve smartest people on Earth, and Newton would have been by far the smartest! And this is assumed without them even taking an actual intelligence test.

---

[62] 13 Most Intelligent People In The History Of The World - Financesonline.com
[63] What is IQ? | Mensa International
[64] IQ Percentile and Rarity Chart (iqcomparisonsite.com)
[65] World Population by Year - Worldometer (worldometers.info)

VII

Moon landings and space travel

Neil Armstrong was one of my boyhood idols after watching the moon landing on a 12" black-and-white television. I thought, as millions of others did, that Armstrong was a world-class astronaut hero. *He was me* when I played with my toy rocket. I still remember my grandmother's words, "Look down, Eddy, Neil Armstrong ties his shoes."

Historic moon landings are touted as a sign of America's technological superiority. Television documentaries and history books in America also point the finger at many other nations for using propagandized achievements as a way of proving their system's superiority. Ironically, there is plenty of circumstantial evidence pointing to the moon landings as fitting the latter. There is plenty of tangible proof, too.

During a NASA 20-year moon landing press conference, C-Span showed the three Apollo-11 astronauts. Neil Armstrong, Buzz Aldrin, and Michael Collins.[66] During this session, all three seemed curiously distant and unenthusiastic. Audience eye contact was absent throughout the hour-long session. The body language and facial expressions were akin to the three of them being under cross-examination for a high-level crime. If that statement is too strong, then I would suggest that, at the very least, the three

---

[66] 20th Anniversary of Apollo 11 Flight | C-SPAN.org

astronauts screamed of disingenuousness. I ask the reader to view this press conference and judge for themself.

Next up: The most famous phone call ever. President Nixon spoke to Buzz Aldrin a quarter of a million miles away, on a landline? With no delay? The speed of sound in the air is 767mph.[67]

Then there's the Apollo 11 moon lander that looks like a collection of tin foil, tape, hangers, cardboard, papier mâché, and warped paneling that supposedly traveled several times the speed of a bullet and withstood hundreds of degrees of temperature fluctuations. I invite the reader to look at the picture.[68]

Could the greatest achievement in the history of mankind be a great achievement for a different reason? Ever wonder what mankind's biggest achievement would be if the moon landings were a hoax? Second honors would move into first. According to one article, creating electronic devices would then occupy the top spot.[69]

Perhaps the biggest clue for invalidation is the fact that the last moon landing allegedly occurred over a half-century ago. The reasons for not going back are at best confusing. Newsweek's article here explained 20 reasons why we haven't gone back. Number #16 caught my eye because it is titled "unreliable technology." Moonquakes, temperature extremes, craters made from constant asteroid collisions, micrometeorites, "space junk," and here is #20: According

---

[67] Speed of sound - Wikipedia
[68] Lunar Module Eagle - Wikipedia
[69] Top 10 Greatest Achievements of Mankind - TheTopTens

to television media and official government sources, astronauts landed on the moon a half-century ago. In 50+ years, we have not gone back. The excuse used by NASA astronaut Don Petit was, "I'd go to the moon in a nanosecond. The problem is we don't have the technology to do that anymore. We used to, but we destroyed that technology, and it's a painful process to build it back again."[70]

The fact of the matter is, the proof of moon landings probably does not even qualify as scant evidence. Richard Nixon was president during all of the supposed trips to the moon. How many people even remember his vice president? His name was Spiro Agnew. Since that presidency, every subsequent administration has only bragged about the technological advancements made under Nixon. Ford, Carter, Reagan, Bush, Clinton, Bush, Obama, Trump, and Biden can all proudly claim they have not only not taken the baton from Nixon, but they lost it in the exchange!

---

[70] NASA: We're No Longer Able To Visit The Moon - News Punch

VIII

Pictures and Images

It seems there is some kind of "don't ask/don't tell" policy when it comes to getting authentic photos or video clips of the spinning ball earth from alleged space missions. Of the many trips these space agencies have made, you'd think they should have libraries full of albums full of photographs of Earth. And what about videos? If this is more than we could expect for ROI, then there should be at least hundreds of legitimate photos available to the tax-paying public, right? Dozens? Nope. Multiply any number by zero, and that's how many photographs there are of a ball Earth from space. Images, yes. Photographs, no. Does NASA nix all cameras before their space adventures?

A picture forms an image. However, an image can be created, and a photograph is an authentic picture.

Photograph: anything taken by a camera or photocopier. **Image**: any visual object that's modified or altered by a computer or an imaginary object created using a computer. **Picture**: a drawing, painting, or artwork, computer creation, or even a photograph.

A picture is worth a thousand words. Pictures convey information at the speed of sight. Emotions can arise instantly when seeing the photograph of a child's smiling face on Christmas, or the shock he has after opening a gift. Telling a friend about how nice your trip to Puerto Rico was would likely not convey as vividly as showing him a picture of the clear blue water off the ocean beach. Pictures may also serve more surreptitious purposes.

The famous *Blue Marble* is an ever-changing computer-generated image. That's right, image – not photograph. The picture (image) was supposedly taken during a moon mission in 1972 at a distance of 18,000 miles from Earth.[71]

If satellites existed in space and the Earth was a spinning ball, it's more than reasonable to assume we should have legitimate photographs of Earth to prove it. No camera from a satellite has ever zoomed in on a car driving upside down. No photos or videos of planes flying upside down and sideways, either.

Satellites are alleged to fly in the thermosphere, where temperatures routinely exceed 4,000 degrees Fahrenheit.[72] However, the metals used on satellites cannot withstand much more than half of that heat. Satellites are alleged to transmit signals over much greater geographical areas than conventional television and radio systems. If that were true, it would raise an important question: why would we need radio towers, or undersea cables, for that matter?

Navigating the NASA website, one will find photographs of NASA crews on Earth, yet only enhanced images of their supposed findings in outer space.[73]

---

[71] The Blue Marble - Wikipedia
[72] Facts About The Thermosphere: What It Is, And Its Defining Characteristics (ownyourweather.com)
[73] NASA Images - NASA

Pictures can be faked or doctored. Governments are notorious for propagandizing pictures. There are some telltale signs that pictures are not authentic, even when created by techno-savvy engineers. However, the job of detection is not always an easy one. The Defense Advanced Research Projects Agency (DARPA) is trying to create a tool to automatically detect if a picture came from a camera or was fooled with. The possibility of developing something that can detect phonies 100% of the time is not likely, however.[74] Still, it will be interesting to see how much this technology is used on expensive government agencies like NASA.

---

[74] The hidden signs that can reveal a fake photo - BBC Future

IX

Sun and moon

According to its spectral class, the Sun is a G-type main-sequence star (G2V). As such, it is informally, and not completely accurately, referred to as a yellow dwarf (its light is closer to white than yellow). It formed approximately 4.6 billion[a][14][22] years ago from the gravitational collapse of matter within a region of a large molecular cloud. Most of this matter gathered in the center, whereas the rest flattened into an orbiting disk that became the Solar System. The central mass became so hot and dense that it eventually initiated nuclear fusion in its core. It is thought that almost all stars form by this process.[75]

The above Wikipedia entry for the sun is rather incomprehensible. Most people won't read, understand, or ever be able to repeat it verbatim. They will skim through it and simply assume it is well-researched and proven. Contradictorily, however, flat Earth logic is not so confusing.

Flat-Earthers believe that the sun and moon move in circular motion above a flat, stationary Earth. This is how we have our days and nights. The 24-hour day is the time it takes the sun to complete one revolution around Earth.

Science was the only elementary class in which I received an A+. Many nights during my summer vacations were spent looking at the stars and planets with my father

---

[75] Sun - Wikipedia

and brothers. My father would point out Mercury and Venus. Absent from my mind was an awareness that if the Earth were a spinning ball, and we were on the side opposite the sun, we would not be able to see the two planets alleged to be between the Earth and Sun!

The accepted – not by flat-Earthers – distance between Earth and Sun is 93 million miles. Since we have no practical way to measure the sun, we can assume its size is relative to its distance from Earth. If the sun were millions of miles away and occupied the amount of space in the sky that it does, then it would be enormous in comparison to the Earth. However, if the sun were local, it would be much smaller. Eric Dubay's Flat Earth Proof #122 discusses how plane trigonometry from flat-Earthers throughout the ages calculates the sun and moon to both be about 32 miles in diameter.[76] Using intermediate-level mathematical calculations, the sun's distance from Earth is calculated to be in the 3000-mile range.[77]

Also, why would there be such a disparity in temperatures on different parts of the Earth if the sun (Earth's heat source) is 93 million miles away? After all, the Earth is alleged to be only a tiny fraction of the size of the Sun. In a flat, stationary Earth model with a local sun and moon rotating between the Tropic of Capricorn and the Tropic of Cancer, the polar regions would logically be much colder. However, there is a huge disparity in average temperatures between Antarctica, and the Arctic. The North

---

[76] FE Proofs - Part 3 (flatearth101.com)
[77] Mathematical proof the sun is not 93 million miles away – STOP | LOOK | THINK (stoplookthink.com)

Pole averages are 32° F (Summer), -40° F (Winter); the South Pole is -18° F (Summer), -76° F (Winter).[78] This corroborates the model of a flat, stationary Earth with a moving sun. The 24-hour day cycle spends less time on the south-facing surface because of the much larger south circle. The sun doesn't spend as much time per square of surface area over Antarctica (the Earth's outer perimeter).

Most flat Earth models show a moon and sun approximately the same size and distance from Earth. The official government claim is that the moon is about 238,900 miles from Earth.[79]

The moon is said to be a spherical body made up of rock. However, there are many instances when you can look right through it as though it is a non-body luminary.

"NASA and modern astronomy maintain that the Moon is a solid, spherical, Earth-like habitation which man has actually flown to and set foot on. They claim the Moon is a non-luminescent planetoid which receives and reflects all its light from the Sun. The reality is, however, that the Moon is not a solid body, it is clearly circular, but not spherical, and not in any way an Earth-like planetoid which humans could set foot on. In fact, the Moon is largely transparent and completely self-luminescent, shining with its own unique light." – Eric Dubay.[80]

---

[78] Which pole is colder? | NASA Climate Kids
[79] Moon - Wikipedia
[80] fake moon landing – Liberty & Justice For All (wordpress.com)

X

Gravity

Gravity is the widely accepted reason why everything falls to Earth. Though it makes a tiny bit of sense, this concept is taught as factual rather than unproven. Density and buoyancy are simpler ways of explaining why something would fall from the sky, float, or sink. Gravity on a ball-Earth has many unanswerable questions. Gravity holds giant skyscrapers to the Earth upside-down and sideways, but won't pull down a butterfly or a balloon? Another counter-argument for the alleged awesome strength of gravity is the magnet test. One can take a small magnet and pick up a piece of metal off the ground from above it. The metal will stay stuck to the magnet, proving the magnet is stronger than the force of gravity.

If not for an appeal to authority (fallacy), there would not be an explanation for how gravity could cause the Earth's oceans to stay stuck to a spinning ball. In reality, gravity is a mythical pulling force that may be deliberately not explainable.

I was taught in elementary school that Sir Isaac Newton discovered gravity. An apple fell from a tree above him and hit him in the head. This genius then concluded the Earth must be a giant spinning ball. Gravity is the lifeblood of the spinning-ball Earth story. Gravity can be described but not explained. Gravity is at best a weak hypothesis.

XI

Media & Government – Again!

Celebrities

Flat-Earthers believe their arguments are very valid, but when noted celebrities come on board, the movement spikes in popularity. This is especially true when the celebrities publicly acknowledge their beliefs.

A CBS Sports article by Kyle Boone (February 17, 2017) is titled: *Kyrie Irving says the Earth is undeniably flat: 'This is not even a conspiracy theory.'*

"This is not even a conspiracy theory," Irving said. "The Earth is flat."

When pressed on a response that, for the record, is flat out wrong, Irving went off the rails and blamed "particular groups" that he did not name, which he thinks want to convince us the Earth is, in fact, round.

Said Irving: "It's right in front of our faces. I'm telling you, it's right in front of our faces. They lie to us.

"What I've been taught is that the earth is round. But if you really think about it from a landscape of the way we travel, the way we move and the fact that, can you really think of us rotating around the sun and all planets aligned, rotating in specific dates, being perpendicular with what's going on with these planets?"

Almost in disbelief with his sincere response, Richard Jefferson asked: "How are you going to put the word 'planets' in quotations?"

"Because, everything that they send — or that they want to say they're sending — doesn't come back," Irving reasoned. "There is no concrete information except for the information that they're giving us. They're particularly putting you in the direction of what to believe and what not to believe. The truth is right there, you just got to go searching for it."[81]

In a related February 2017 article, the great NBA player Irving told his teammates, "The Earth is flat." At the end of the article, the author states that Kyrie Irving doubled down on [his beliefs] by adding a video clip. The clip shows Irving saying, "People should do their own research and either back my belief or throw it in the water." Kyrie is then asked if he's seen pictures of Earth, and he says he's seen a lot of things that his educational system says are real that turned out to be completely fake. He added that he doesn't mind going against the grain in his beliefs.[82]

The obvious bias that is presented is that the article never focuses on the fact that Irving suggests that people should do their own research, but continues to push the notion that the flat-Earth theory is hoax news.

---

[81] Kyrie Irving says the Earth is undeniably flat: 'This is not even a conspiracy theory' - CBSSports.com
[82] Kyrie Irving reveals he believes the Earth is flat, believes in other conspiracy theories | RSN (nbcsports.com)

A year-plus after Irving's media splash, headlines came out about how Irving apologized for "spreading his wild flat-earth theory."[83] Of course, this gives the viewer the impression that (a) Irving was not serious about the Earth being flat, and (b) Flat-earth theory is absurd. However, Irving never said he doesn't believe the Earth is flat, and encouraged individuals to do independent research. The fact that the media pressured Irving to retract should raise red flags. Kyrie Irving was also questioned about his flat-Earth opinion on the Jimmy Kimmel show, and Kimmel handed him a globe, and Kyrie spun the globe on his fingers like a basketball, downplaying the seriousness of a flat-Earth.[84] If the Earth really is flat and that truth is deliberately hidden, it's most reasonable to assume there would be pressure against popular people publicly saying so. If flat-Earth was a wild conspiracy with zero substance, why would anybody complain and make it newsworthy?

Another all-time great NBA player, Shaquille O'Neal, corroborated Irving's story in 2017. He has since retracted his original statements. In a confusing back-and-forth article, O'Neal is quoted as saying that when he talks, 80% of the time, he is being humorous, and 20% of the time, he is being serious.[85]

Rapper Bobb Ray Simmons (B.o.B) told his 2.3 million Twitter followers he believes the Earth is flat. He said he didn't want to believe it, but was convinced upon accepting

---

[83] Celtics Kyrie Irving sorry for spreading flat-Earth theory (yahoo.com)
[84] Kyrie Irving on Flat Earth Theory, LeBron James & NBA All-Star Game - YouTube
[85] Unfortunately, Shaquille O'Neal isn't actually a flat-Earther: 'I'm joking, you idiots' (yahoo.com)

certain facts, such as Earth's horizon never leaving upon high altitude ascension. He blames mass media for the deception and encourages independent research. He tweeted out from his Twitter account – if my tweets are rattling the tiny little cages of your reality ... the unfollow button is right there.[86]

Of course, there is a price to pay for having a dissident socio-scientific belief. In a 2018 article by Joey Haverford, there are 10 celebrity flat-Earthers assorted with 10 other celebrities who believe in "seriously odd other things." The article's intent is to juxtapose flat-Earthers with the bizarre. The first paragraph predictably begins with calling the flat-Earth movement absurd:

One of the seemingly inconceivable and controversial theories to gain popularity in recent years is the belief that the Earth is flat. Science and history say otherwise, with a lot of facts that should prevent the Flat Earth theory from reaching the mainstream level. However, many people have their own reasons as to why they think the Earth is flat.[87]

Some of the celebrities are totally rational, some are far-fetched. Here are some excerpts:

Kyrie Irving: Flat Earth MVP.

Miley Cyrus: claims ghosts live on her sink.

---

[86] Rapper B.o.B thinks the Earth is flat and he's got photos to prove it | CNN

[87] 10 Celebs Who Actually Believe The Earth Is Flat (10 Who Believe Worse) (thetravel.com)

Kanye West: Past interviews of Kanye West have seen him reference many unique beliefs. One controversial instance of this featured West questioning the shape of the Earth. Kanye has never officially come out as a flat-Earther, but he does certainly have enough questions to show that he's leaning that way.

Emma Stone: Believes ghost of a relative drops quarters in her home.

Stefon Diggs: Quietly revealed his wild belief. This makes it more surprising that someone as commendable as Diggs can get coaxed into believing the Flat Earth theory. Diggs made it known publicly on social media that he agreed with NBA star Kyrie Irving that the Earth is flat.

Tila Tequila – But She Says Anything For Attention. Tila Tequila found fame during the social media internet rise allowing average folks to develop followings. The reputation of Tequila is not credible as she has been known to play things up to find popularity online.

Whoopi Goldberg: Thinks the moon landing was staged.

Draymond Green: One reason given by Green for his theory is that he can make pictures round with his iPhone today, so he doesn't trust any scientific evidence of the shape of the planet.

Kylie Jenner: Believes In Chem Trails.

Dan Akroyd: Thinks Aliens are watching Mick Jagger Dance.

Terrence Howard: Believes math is wrong.

Sherri Shepherd: Comedian and talk show host Sherri Shepherd was in the public spotlight for suggesting the Flat Earth theory was indeed accurate a few years ago. Shepherd has been a part of the highly successful talk show - The View. Many of the hot-button topics are discussed on the show, and Shepherd let it slip that she believed the Earth may be flat.

A future statement featured Shepherd claiming she was just nervous discussing the topic and she accepts the science behind the Earth being round. However, the initial questions speculating if the Earth was flat seemed more authentic from her than the backtracking.

Lala Kent: Believes Tupac is living within her soul.

What this article really accomplishes is to help make flat-earth believers' part of a community of outsiders. By outsiders, I mean the psychologically irrational irritants. The article listed the 20 celebrities numerically, with all of the odd numbers (10 of them) being flat-earthers.

The US Congress found flat-Earth content so disturbing that they found it necessary to cross-examine tech giants on their policies.[88] Nothing like an indirect compliment to the exponentially growing movement!

In an early 2019 article, Google-owned YouTube stated it would start censoring content: "To that end, we'll begin reducing recommendations of borderline content and content that could misinform users in harmful ways," YouTube said in a blog post. "Such as videos promoting a phony miracle cure for a serious illness, claiming the earth

---

[88] Congress Questions Facebook, YouTube over Censorship (Flat Earth)

is flat, or making blatantly false claims about historic events like 9/11."[89] Videos on miracle cures can theoretically cause death and illness, and 9/11 is an intensely serious subject to the extent that there was an official government 9/11 Commission report compiled a year after the event.[90] Again, juxtaposition in order to defame the growing flat-Earth movement.

The following is an interesting abstract and conclusion from Vol 8, No 2 (2020): Health and Science Controversies in the Digital World: News, Mis/Disinformation and Public Engagement

[Abstract] Calls for censorship have been made in response to the proliferation of flat Earth videos on YouTube, but these videos are likely convincing to very few. Instead, people may worry that these videos are brainwashing others. That individuals believe other people will be more influenced by media messages than themselves is called third-person perception (TPP), and the consequences from those perceptions, such as calls for censorship, are called third-person effects (TPE). Here, we conduct three studies that examine the flat Earth phenomenon using TPP and TPE as a theoretical framework. We first measured participants' own perceptions of the convincingness of flat Earth arguments presented in YouTube videos and compared these to participants' perceptions of how convincing others might find the arguments. Instead of merely looking at ratings of one's self vs. a general 'other,' however, we asked people to consider a variety of identity groups who differ based on

---

[89] YouTube demotes flat-earthers, conspiracy theorists (phys.org)
[90] The 9/11 Commission Report (9-11commission.gov)

political party, religiosity, educational attainment, and area of residence (e.g., rural, urban). We found that participants' religiosity and political party were the strongest predictors of TPP across the different identity groups. In our second and third pre-registered studies, we found support for our first study's conclusions, and we found mixed evidence for whether TPP predicts support for censoring YouTube among the public.

[Conclusion] Because YouTube recently announced modifications to its recommendation algorithms and specifically mentioned flat Earth in its announcement (YouTube, 2019), it is evident that the management at YouTube is concerned about the influence of these videos on the public. Undoubtedly, YouTube was facing public pressure to take some action as a result of recent issues, such as articles blaming YouTube's algorithms for the rise in flat Earthers and promotion of other conspiracies, like QAnon (Coaston, 2018). Presumably, those who support regulation of such content, as well as YouTube's upper management who implemented these regulations, hold strong TPP, and they may have overestimated the effects these videos would have on others. Though our research only partially supports the theory that the general public would support censoring flat Earth videos on YouTube based on their own TPP, such perceptions may have played a significant role in these executives' decision making.[91]

Banning something based on "third-party perception" seems more than a bit odd. This definitely seems like a dance

---

[91] MaC 8(2) - Third-Person Perceptions and Calls for Censorship of Flat Earth Videos on YouTube (1).pdf

around the fact that the flat-Earth movement is growing, and FE arguments are making believers out of way more than "very few." The censorship fits the definition of damage control on the part of YouTube's ownership.

Flat-Earth theory is not exactly hate speech either. I have seen hours and hours of flat-Earth documentaries and read hundreds of articles and a few books as well. Not a word was mentioned suggesting violence or illegality in any way. Therefore, hate and illegality can be ruled out as grounds for censorship. Even putting an age restriction on flat-Earth videos would not be necessary if the concepts were extremely far-fetched.

Digressing back to television, the whole concept of modern media caring about what impressionable young viewers watch holds nearly zero merit. Whilst aggressively censoring flat-Earthers, the media pours out countless scenes of deadly violence, infidelity, and an array of criminal activity every day. The average child sees 12,000 violent acts on television annually, including many depictions of murder and rape. Sexual relations between unmarried partners occur 24 times more often than between spouses.[92]

---

[92] Children and the media - PMC (nih.gov)

XII

Antarctic Treaty

Imagine if every military power in the world collectively joined forces to establish a super-superpower. In order for this to happen, the entire world would have to be in grave danger. Would it even be possible for nations at war with one another to become cooperatives?

Enter the Antarctic Treaty.

Promoting peaceful cooperation in the nearly populationless land of Antarctica is far more important than human trafficking, economic collapses, and perennial wars everywhere else. Just in case you didn't catch it, that was sarcasm.

A solid way to test Earth's shape is to measure how far you travel when you circle the globe in the southern hemisphere and compare it to the same kind of trip in the northern hemisphere. If Earth is a sphere like the well-known Blue Marble photo shows, distances at the same north and south latitudes should match. In the globe model, the equator is the widest point, with a circumference of about 25,000 miles. If Earth is round, the distance around should get smaller as you move toward either pole. If Earth were a flat disk, the distance would only get larger as you go farther south.

In sharp contrast to the famous circular Blue Marble image, the "astrophysicist experts" claim the Earth is pear-shaped. This indirect admission (The Blue Marble is a composite and not a 1972 NASA photograph) is likely due to the fact that the southern hemisphere can be independently measured between the equator and 60° south latitude. If the southern hemisphere gradually widens, which it does, the Earth is not a perfect ball shape and could be shaped like a disk pending further southern measurements. However, trips further south (beyond 60 degrees south latitude) are forbidden by all significant world militaries. Therefore, they can cling to the pear-shape – for now.

Somehow, all nations want to protect a land that nobody can fly over at the bottom of the globe because it's too cold and inhospitable? Also of note, no government or independent plane has ever flown south over Antarctica and finished their trip on the other side of the alleged globular Earth. Flat-Earthers maintain that this is because these flights are not possible. After all, Antarctica is the perimeter of the disk-shaped flat Earth.

The Antarctic Treaty was established in 1959 and rarely receives attention in the classroom or the media. So much so that most people are not even aware that this treaty exists. Curiously enough, the space race began its exponential growth phase in the 1960s, with all the attention diverted from lateral exploration to vertical exploration. Though the timeline of the Antarctic Treaty falls on the circumstantial evidence side of the flat-earth argument, it still begs the question of why can't peaceful people explore there?

The Antarctic Treaty, curiously enough, encompasses 54 different states. Here are just a few: the USA, Canada, the United Kingdom, Russia, Ukraine, Germany, Italy, France,

Spain, Australia, Brazil, Argentina, China, Japan, India, Pakistan, North Korea, South Korea, et al.[93] Notice the daily hostilities these countries engage in against one another, yet they all come together to militarily guard exploration below 60 degrees south latitude.

Note the following from the Antarctic Report website:

The Antarctic Treaty applies to the entire region south of 60° South Latitude. It effectively stops nations from making territorial claims or from exploiting Antarctic resources.

The Antarctic Treaty was negotiated by 12 countries in 1959: Argentina, Australia, Belgium, Chile, France, Japan, New Zealand, Norway, South Africa, UK, USA and USSR.

The fundamental aim of the Antarctic Treaty is that Antarctica "shall continue forever to be used exclusively for peaceful purposes and shall not become the scene or object of international discord". It prohibits military activity and allows for "freedom of scientific investigation in Antarctica, promote international cooperation in scientific investigation in Antarctica" and mandates detailed information to be exchanges.[94]

Again, why such a cooperative effort to police the deep freeze? As mentioned previously, the joint policing would prevent any independent investigation to conclusively prove exactly how many miles there are in order to circumnavigate Antarctica. Perhaps there are some other reasons multiple

---

[93] Antarctic Treaty System - Wikipedia
[94] What is the Antarctic Treaty? (antarcticreport.com)

governments forbid Antarctic exploration. There are those who cite an interview with Admiral Byrd, where he claimed there was land beyond the Antarctic ice wall that had an amazing abundance of natural resources.[95] If this is true, the motivation could be monetary and economic control. Colluding governments would each get to maintain their financial advantage over their respective populations.

By process of elimination, there is an ulterior reason that all the major militaries jointly patrol Antarctica. Before, during, and after the Antarctica Treaty, we have been living alongside worldwide volatility with the most formidable militaries pointing guns at each other. Countless wars have taken place during the last century, so why are all these nations so concerned with making Antarctica forever peaceful? Perhaps some countries want peace indefinitely, but worrying about keeping a barren Iceland at peace is quite simply not worth that kind of military investment.

Another international body developed post-World War 2 was the United Nations (UN). Their purpose was to maintain international peace. Despite all the favorable press the UN has received, it failed at its primary objective. Like most government-subsidized orgs, they have managed to stay funded despite this. The UN started with 51 nations aboard, and has grown to 193.[96] Interestingly enough, the UN uses the flat Earth map as its emblem.[97]

---

[95] You Must Watch What Admiral Byrd Said About Antarctica FULL interview (2020) - YouTube
[96] United Nations - Wikipedia
[97] Emblem of the United Nations - United Nations - Wikipedia

XIII

The Flat-Earth model:

The Earth is a flat, level plain. Oceans and all standing bodies of water are proven to be level, and not bent to a convex shape. Man's original concept of Earth was that it was flat. This was the status quo throughout history until about 500 years ago.

The perimeter (circumference) of the Earth is Antarctica, while the interior of the disk-shaped Earth is the Arctic. Antarctica is an ice wall approximately 150-200 feet high that holds the oceans inside. Not too much else is known about Antarctica due to the lack of exploration. The lack of exploration has practical reasons, but collective government enforcement has so far halted any would-be explorers who wished to tough it out. The North Star does not move and is directly above the center of our Earth realm, the North Pole.

The Earth is motionless. It is not spinning 1,000mph and does not rotate around the sun. This is exactly what man originally believed because it is exactly what our senses tell us. The sun, moon, and all stars except the North Star move around the Earth. The planets, stars, sun, and moon are not spheres; they are most likely luminaries. The sun and the moon are much closer to the Earth than our encyclopedias and media claim. The sun and the moon are approximately the same size.

Space as a vacuum doesn't exist, and we have never landed on the moon. There is either a firmament or some type of shield that prevents vertical travel past a certain point. What is beyond the height of this shield is speculative because it has never been explored or even reached.

Moon landings were faked, as are all alleged trips into outer space, including satellites and space stations. NASA and other space agencies are filled with liars and actors at the top. NASA's proofs are CGI images, green screens, and other visual tricks. Governments all over the world corroborate the lies for surreptitious reasons. Many are paid off to look the other way, but the core of the lies comes from a source demanding control. There is a super-wealthy core cabal that keeps the true facts of Earth from the public. To do so, they manipulate their control of the means of mass communication.

Much of the indoctrination involves financial gains. Government agencies collect billions, if not trillions of dollars, for lies. Their willing collaborators either don't know or don't care about much other than compensation and temporary prestige.

It appears that the wealthy cabal fears that if the masses revert to their natural senses, they (Cabal) will lose power. Moreover, they won't be able to retrieve their power anytime soon. Perhaps not ever again. The truth of the flat Earth will eventually prevail.

This hand-drawn illustration is far closer to what the Earth looks like from above than any globe in any classroom:

Polaris (North Star) sits directly over Earth's center and remains motionless.

Earth is surrounded by a 200-foot ice wall, which keeps the Earth's waters contained. The sun and the moon revolve around the stationary Earth, traveling from the Tropic of Capricorn (Winter solstice) to pass the Equator (Equinox twice a year) to the Tropic of Cancer (Summer solstice).

Conclusion

This adventure down the rabbit hole began with a look at the media, the one with the rapid trust depreciation problem. Ditto the government. Further down the journey is the medical industry, where extending the lives of sick people takes priority over cures. Shortly thereafter, the trip hits turbulence. Religion is set apart from the ordinary. However, the rabbit hole only contends that the failure to separate religion from spirituality is intentional. Scrutinizing hierarchical religion does not seek to disconnect people from their destiny, nor does it conclude that we are not infinite beings. What lies even deeper in the metaphorical rabbit hole is the fact that our cosmology has been hidden from us for centuries.

The democratic standard of at least 51% now understands that deception is embedded in society's present arrangement. We have been teased by conspiracies for decades, with many existing only on the fringe. However, conspiracy theories have received more attention in recent years for three reasons. 1) The Internet has exponentially expanded worldwide communications. 2) The media and the government's habitual lies chase people to the fringe. 3) Some of these "conspiracy theories" have more substance than flash. Media, government, banks, healthcare, organized religion, and science are symbiotic businesses. If these were truly useful, we would have accurate news of important happenings, very little crime, no wars, economic stability, good health, good spirit, and the ability to question science.

At present, people are still complying with a corrupt system. The mortal enemy of corruption is the truth. Is there a truth so powerful that the system of external control cannot handle it? There is a lie so powerful that authoritarianism will be rendered useless once it is shared enough times. The lie is that the Earth is a spinning ball rather than the immovable center of creation. A lie that no government official, educator, scientist, or television network can quietly withdraw from.

The JFK assassination has simmered in the minds of Americans for over six decades. Many people also believe that 9-11 was an inside job. The post-World War II wars have turned out to be mistakes. An ever-growing national deficit has created a financial bubble under the guise of national defense as well as social programs. Big Pharma pimps their drugs on television, radio, and all over the Internet. These mistakes are forgiven and forgotten because the political theatre has parties blaming each other. This option is still available to the government as a whole. Isolating one party as the sole proprietor of a flat Earth is impossible.

Once you accept that the Earth is flat and stationary, you agree that primary, secondary, and higher education are cosmologically useless. You also agree that Eratosthenes, Copernicus, Newton, and Einstein were frauds. You agree that the television and media 24/7 reminders that we live on a planet are wrongful deceptions. You agree that the Earth is not the product of an accidental Big Bang. You agree that it is not accidentally taught as such.

The current sociological system is beyond reconciliation. The paradigm shift is now available in pill form, red.

Author Bio

Edward Spiro Bicker is a political activist, community volunteer, former city councilman, and college math tutor. He has well over 30 years of experience as a union worker, 20 years as a supervisor, and 3 years as a shop steward. Edward has an MBA and is a member of *Delta Mu Delta* international honor society. He adheres to a body, mind, and spirit fitness regimen.

"A candle loses nothing by lighting another candle." *James Keller*